THE
STATE
STRIKES
BACK

THE END OF
ECONOMIC REFORM
IN CHINA?

NICHOLAS R. LARDY

THE STATE STRIKES BACK

THE END OF ECONOMIC REFORM IN CHINA?

Peterson Institute for International Economics

Washington, DC

January 2019

Nicholas R. Lardy, called "everybody's guru on China" by the *National Journal*, is the Anthony M. Solomon Senior Fellow at the Peterson Institute for International Economics. He joined the Institute in March 2003 from the Brookings Institution, where he was a senior fellow from 1995 until 2003. He was the director of the Henry M. Jackson School of International Studies at the University of Washington from 1991 to 1995. From 1997 through the spring of 2000, he was also the Frederick Frank Adjunct Professor of International Trade and Finance at the Yale University School of Management. He is author, coauthor, or editor of numerous books, including *Markets over Mao: The Rise of Private Business in China* (2014), *Sustaining China's Economic Growth after the Global Financial Crisis* (2012), *The Future of China's Exchange Rate Policy* (2009), *China's Rise: Challenges and Opportunities* (2008), *Debating China's Exchange Rate Policy* (2008), and *China: The Balance Sheet—What the World Needs to Know Now about the Emerging Superpower* (2006). Lardy is a member of the Council on Foreign Relations and of the editorial boards of *Asia Policy* and the *China Review*.

**PETERSON INSTITUTE FOR
INTERNATIONAL ECONOMICS**
1750 Massachusetts Avenue, NW
Washington, DC 20036-1903
+1.202.328.9000 www.piie.com

Adam S. Posen, President
Steven R. Weisman, Vice President for
  Publications and Communications

Cover Design by Peggy Archambault

Library of Congress Cataloging-in-Publication Data
Name: Lardy, Nicholas R., author. Title: The state strikes back : the end of economic reform in China? Nicholas R. Lardy. Description: Washington, DC : Peterson Institute for International Economics, [2019] Includes bibliographical references and index.

Identifiers: LCCN 2018039390 (print)
LCCN 2018056104 (ebook)

ISBN 9780881327373 (paper)
ISBN 9780881327380 (ebook)

Subjects: LCSH: China—Economic policy—2000– | China—Economic conditions—2000–

Classification: LCC HC427.95 (ebook) | LCC HC427.95 .L369 2019 (print) | DDC 338.951—dc23.

This publication has been subjected to a prepublication peer review intended to ensure analytical quality. The views expressed are those of the author. This publication is part of the overall program of the Peterson Institute for International Economics, as endorsed by its Board of Directors, but it does not necessarily reflect the views of individual members of the Board or of the Institute's staff or management.

The Peterson Institute for International Economics is a private nonpartisan, nonprofit institution for rigorous, intellectually open, and indepth study and discussion of international economic policy. Its purpose is to identify and analyze important issues to make globalization beneficial and sustainable for the people of the United States and the world, and then to develop and communicate practical new approaches for dealing with them. Its work is funded by a highly diverse group of philanthropic foundations, private corporations, and interested individuals, as well as income on its capital fund. About 35 percent of the Institute's resources were provided by contributors from outside the United States. A list of all financial supporters is posted at https://piie.com/sites/default/files/supporters.pdf.

Contents

Appendices

References   143

Index   155

Tables

Box

Figures

Preface

The range of views expressed on the likely future pace of China's economic growth is stunningly wide. Some contend that in terms of common prices China's GDP already exceeds that of the United States and project that it will soon overtake the United States even measured at market prices. Others are equally confident that China's growth over the next decade or two will slow to an average rate of only two to three percent, a pace not much above the likely trajectory of the United States. Both camps, and many in between, treat their projections as predetermined by great forces—whether the oft-mentioned but dubious "middle-income trap" pushing the trend relentlessly down, or the sheer size and nature of China's global presence keeping the growth rate up high.

Rightly and powerfully, Nicholas Lardy argues that China's economic trajectory is far from predestined. Instead, the Chinese state's policy choices will be the major determinant of its future growth. The slowdown of recent years is not primarily the natural slowing of what is now a more mature, upper middle-income country. It reflects the increasing drag of state companies on economic growth and the burgeoning misallocation of resources by China's financial sector. If China's leadership continues to opt for state-led growth in pursuit of greater economic and political control, China's growth trend would slow further. Alternatively, if China's leadership goes back to a market-oriented reform program, that would boost China's trend growth to well above the pace of recent years. In this study, Lardy not only demonstrates the economic costs to China—and to the world—of the state having struck back since 2011 but he also outlines a path that would sustainably raise China's growth rate. The economic benefits to China and the world would be enormous, but it would require the reduction of some control reimposed by the Chinese state over the economy.

Any longer-term projection must be based on a deep understanding of the contingent factors and policy choices that account for the recent slowdown in China's growth, from the double-digit pace in the decade through 2011 to the 6 to 7 percent range since that time. Lardy's analysis shows that a main driving factor was the turn away from the market orientation that guided economic reform for more than three decades starting in 1978. Market-oriented reform based on private firms was wildly successful. By 2012 these firms accounted for 70 percent of China's output, up from almost nothing in 1978. But a visible change in strategy, in favor of state led growth, accelerated under the leadership of party Chairman Xi Jinping starting in 2012.

Xi came into office endorsing wide-ranging market-oriented economic reform but he quickly abandoned this design in favor of a more statist approach. This was evident in more aggressive, detailed industrial policies that directed a growing flow of resources to priorities identified by the state; mergers of already large state companies to form even larger conglomerates that reduced competition in many critical sectors; a redirection of credit away from far more productive private firms to underperforming state companies; and an undermining of private property rights that further reduced private investment. But state-led growth clearly has failed in economic terms. The productivity of state firms in industry and services is now two-thirds and two-fifths lower, respectively, than a decade ago, while the productivity of private firms has continued to increase.

Another important contributor to China's economic slowdown is the shift towards sustainable domestic-driven growth. Unlike the return to heavy state intervention, the move to focus on internal growth drivers was both necessary and beneficial. Much of China's growth in the first decade of this century was held above potential by a rapidly expanding trade surplus. This overheating was itself largely driven by an increasingly undervalued exchange rate that significantly inflated aggregate demand. This policy not only garnered substantial international opprobrium making it costly to maintain—it distorted domestic resource allocation contrary to China's own well-being. This policy was gradually but decisively abandoned. Export-driven growth has faded away. At a time when China's international economic impact remains under sharp external criticism, only some of it justified, Lardy contributes a healthy reality-check on excessive claims about the importance of export-led growth to China's past growth and future prospects. While specific trade and investment issues merit serious attention, continued strong Chinese growth is sustainable both internally and externally. What it takes is deliberate domestic economic reform to restore the ascendance of markets over Mao.

The State Strikes Back is Lardy's fourth book for the Peterson Institute. *China in the World Economy* (1994) provided one of the first assessments of China's emergence as a major force in the global economy. *Sustaining China's Economic Growth after the Global Financial Crisis* (2012) not only analyzed China's strong response to the global crisis, which increased its importance as a source of global economic growth, but also examined the policies that would be necessary to sustain that growth. His third book, *Markets over Mao: The Rise of Private Business* (2014) provided a sweeping analysis of the critical role that the market and private firms played in China's rapid growth after 1978. *The State Strikes Back* continues Lardy's pathbreaking work pursuing his independent analysis of Chinese economic development to wherever the research leads, even when the conclusions are at odds with popular simplistic stories.

***

The Peterson Institute for International Economics is a private nonpartisan, nonprofit institution for rigorous, intellectually open, and indepth study and discussion of international economic policy. Its purpose is to identify and analyze important issues to making globalization beneficial and sustainable for the people of the United States and the world and then to develop and communicate practical new approaches for dealing with them.

The Institute's work is funded by a highly diverse group of philanthropic foundations, private corporations, and interested individuals, as well as income on its capital fund. About 35 percent of the Institute resources in our latest fiscal year were provided by contributors from outside the United States. A list of all our financial supporters for the preceding year is posted at https://piie.com/sites/default/files/supporters.pdf.

The Executive Committee of the Institute's Board of Directors bears overall responsibility for the Institute's direction, gives general guidance and approval to its research program, and evaluates its performance in pursuit of its mission. The Institute's President is responsible for the identification of topics that are likely to become important over the medium term (one to three years) that should be addressed by Institute scholars. This rolling agenda is set in close consultation with the Institute's research staff, taking input from its distinguished Board of Directors and other stakeholders.

The President makes the final decision to publish any individual Institute study, following independent internal and external review of the work. Interested readers may access the data and computations underlying Institute publications for research and replication by searching titles at www.piie.com. The Institute hopes that its research and other activities will contribute to building a stronger foundation for international economic policy around the world. We invite readers of these publications to let us know how they think we can best accomplish this objective.

ADAM S. POSEN
President
Peterson Institute for International Economics

Acknowledgments

This book could not have been completed without the outstanding support of Zixuan Huang, former research analyst at the Peterson Institute for International Economics. She oversaw the gathering of the wealth of information, both quantitative and qualitative, that are the basis for the study. She saved me from making various mistakes and made many useful suggestions to improve the analysis.

Members of a study group convened at the Peterson Institute in May 2018 to critique a draft of the initial manuscript, leading to many improvements in the final outcome. This group included Steven Barnett, C. Fred Bergsten, Martin Chorzempa, William R. Cline, Jérémie Cohen-Setton, Robert Dohner, Lee Folger, Joseph E. Gagnon, Morris Goldstein, Carla A. Hills, Yukong Huang, Jin Zhongxia, William C. Lane, Mary Lovely, Rui Mano, Evan Mederios, Marcus Noland, David Rank, Nicolas Véron, and Dan Wright. I also received written comments on the manuscript from Olivier Blanchard, Jasper Hoek, and Frank Rybinski. I have had useful communications on various issues addressed in the manuscript with Andrew Batson, Nicholas Borst, James Alexander Daniel, Arthur Kroeber, Barry Naughton, Thomas Rawski, and Dan Rosen. The final version of the manuscript was peer reviewed by Steven Barnett, Bert Hofman, and Jeromin Zettelmeyer. Steve Weisman, vice president for publications and communications at the Peterson Institute, made a continuing stream of valuable suggestions starting with the draft manuscript and continuing all the way through to the page proofs. He also led the team responsible for editing, production, and design—Madona Devasahayam and Susann Luetjen. Finally, Adam Posen, president of the Peterson Institute, has provided the leadership that has created a congenial and productive research environment.

Introduction

The world has never seen anything like the rise of China from an impoverished and politically unsteady country in 1978 to a confident and ambitious economic superpower 40 years later. Its economy has grown faster for longer than any other country on record, persistently defying widespread warnings of a drastic slowdown that was supposedly to occur at any moment. To date these predictions have not been borne out. China's growth rate has been declining since its peak on the eve of the global financial crisis, but it has continued to make an outsized contribution to powering worldwide economic expansion. The world has become so dependent on Chinese economic growth and stability that analysts around the world carefully analyze even mild fluctuations in its domestic economy, concerned that these could contribute to a recurrence of global financial instability. When China's domestic stock market melted down in 2015 and again in 2018, many experts fretted that the government would once again resort to exchange rate manipulation to lower the value of Chinese currency to drive more exports. More recently international concern also has focused on the unusually large increase in the ratio of domestic credit to GDP, and the supposed attendant financial risks that could flow from a debt crisis. Many experts fear that a resulting domestic financial crisis would spread turmoil in international markets.

China's stellar growth since 1978 has been driven by market-oriented economic reform. In the era before Deng Xiaoping's introduction of market reforms, the state fixed prices for virtually all commodities and products. That regime gave way to prices determined by supply and demand in the market.

The marketplace for factors of production—such as labor and capital—was substantially reformed. The system of job placement run by state agencies yielded to a robust labor market in which workers were able to move from rural to urban areas or within cities and wages were determined by supply and demand—rather than rigidly fixed by the state. Investment, once largely determined by the State Planning Commission and its various successor agencies and financed almost entirely through the state budget, has also been transformed. By 2012 almost half of all investment was undertaken by profit-oriented private firms with financing provided by retained earnings and ever growing access to credit provided by the state-owned banking system. Because of this transformation, by 2012 private firms contributed an estimated 70 percent of China's GDP (Lardy 2014, 94).

Since 2012, however, this picture of private, market-driven growth has given way to a resurgence of the role of the state in resource allocation and a shrinking role for the market and private firms. Increasingly ambitious state industrial policies carried out by bureaucrats and party officials have been directing investment decisions, most notably in the program proclaimed by President Xi Jinping known as "Made in China 2025." This drive has been financed by many government-guided funds, of which the National Integrated Circuit Investment Fund, created in 2014, is perhaps the best known. In 2015, 297 new government-guided funds were created with more than RMB1.5 trillion in capital (Kozul-Wright and Poon 2017). President Xi assumed the office of the General Secretary of the Chinese Communist Party in late 2012. Since then he has consistently championed the role of state companies, arguing these firms "should be supported and not abandoned" (Economy 2018, 118). Local political leaders have been only too happy to follow his lead by leaning on local financial institutions, such as city commercial banks, to prop up under-performing state companies, most of which are administered at the local rather than central level.

This book mobilizes a wealth of data to evaluate this resurgence in the role of the state, applying an analysis of China's medium-term growth potential and the implications of this growth for the global economy.[1] Its core conclusion is that absent significant further economic reform returning China to a path of allowing market forces to allocate resources, China's growth is likely to slow, casting a shadow over its future prospects. Of major importance for the rest of the world newly dependent on China's economic ups and downs, the goal of reducing financial risks, which have accumulated in the years since the

---

1. Potential growth is the rate of growth of output consistent with stable inflation.

global financial crisis, will be far more difficult. Alternatively, a well-designed economic reform program can rescue the world's most populous country from that dubious fate. Such a program would largely eliminate remaining domestic economic distortions foisted on the economy by the state, raising the average returns on the massive quantity of assets still held by state companies toward the average returns earned by private firms. Expanded reform would likely boost China's growth from the recent range of 6 to 7 percent to an average of 8 percent or possibly slightly more. Moreover, the evidence suggests that this higher growth could well be sustained for a couple of decades. This perspective on China's potential economic growth departs from the forecasts of major international financial institutions. The World Bank (2018b), for example, forecasts that China's growth will slow to 6.3 and 6.2 percent in 2019 and 2020, respectively. Similarly, the International Monetary Fund (IMF) forecasts that China's growth will slow from 6.9 percent in 2017 to 6.4 and 6.3 percent in 2019 and 2020, respectively, and then fall to 5.5 percent by 2023 (IMF 2018).

China's growth slowdown since the global financial crisis has puzzled and confounded many analysts. Accordingly, this book opens with an evaluation in chapter 1 of the causes of China's relatively sluggish growth compared to the hyperperformance of the economy that ended in the global financial crisis of 2008–09. Many analysts (e.g., Carl Minzner 2018) argue that China's slowdown is the result of the natural maturing of an economy and that we should now expect permanently lower growth. These economic experts have predicted further slowing in the years ahead. But these prognosticators are looking at the wrong data. In fact, transitory factors—some of which have largely dissipated—account for a large part of the slowdown. The implication of those factors is important: the evidence suggests that further slowing is far from inevitable—and in fact would be unlikely if China resumed the market-oriented reform strategy evident before President Xi came to power. For example, the single most important cause of China's slowing growth is the evolution of its trade balance with the rest of the world, driven by its capacity as an export superpower. Prior to the global financial crisis, China's growth was driven to an above potential rate by rapidly rising, but ultimately unsustainable, external surpluses powered by phenomenal export performance.

Since the global financial crisis, China's trade has declined as a contributor to its growth for two reasons. First, global trade in general has slowed dramatically compared to earlier decades. Second, domestic developments, notably a substantial appreciation of the renminbi and a reduction in China's saving-investment imbalance has reduced the country's trade surpluses to a much more modest, sustainable level. These two developments have pulled China's growth down to a pace below potential. However, this negative factor now has run its courses suggesting, other things being equal, that China's growth might pick up slightly in coming years.

The second most important contributor to China's slowing economic growth, this book argues, is the slowing pace of domestic economic reform and the resurgence of the role of the state in resource allocation. These trends stifled the competitive forces that had previously powered the Chinese economy, placing more investment in poorly performing and indeed deteriorating state-owned enterprises. Pumping resources into these ailing entities has slowed investment by more productive private firms. Over the entire reform era beginning in 1978 the contribution of state firms to China's growth has shrunk as the private sector has expanded. But since the global financial crisis state firms nonetheless have dragged China's growth down. These ailing enterprises have weakened China's overall economic performance and crowded out investment by far more productive private firms. Chapter 1 cites several other potential contributors to China's slowing growth, ranging from demographics to an inability to move away from an investment and export-driven pattern of growth toward one more reliant on consumption and services. But these other factors are much less important in slowing China's growth than the inhibiting dominance of the state in the economy.

Chapter 2 assesses China's economic growth potential in light of the convergence hypothesis. While China has had extraordinarily rapid growth for more than three decades, by 2014 it was only at about one-quarter of the level of per capita development relative to the frontier, i.e., the level of per capita economic development of the United States as measured by purchasing power parity (i.e., using a "basket of goods" approach to comparing economic performance between countries). This is the same level of economic development recorded vis-à-vis the United States by Japan in 1951, Singapore in 1967, Taiwan in 1975, and South Korea in 1977. Each of these economies subsequently grew rapidly for 20 years or more, in the process strongly converging toward levels of economic development in the United States. Thus, China now falls well short of the relative level of development achieved by these four Asian economies at the end of their two-decade periods of rapid growth. Moreover, the huge disparities in the performance of state firms compared with that of private firms also suggests that there is potential for further convergence in China. These disparities are evident in large and growing differentials between state and private firms in the extent of loss making, the reliance on subsidies, the return on assets, the ratio of debt to equity (the leverage ratio), and the burden of interest payments relative to earnings before taxes and interest.

The chapter rejects the argument of some Chinese officials and economists that state firms are just as efficient as private firms but that they face different constraints that lead to predictably weaker economic performance as measured, for example, by return on assets. The chapter ends with an analysis of the large magnitude of assets controlled by state companies. The evidence demonstrates that if the return on assets of these companies, instead of falling after the global financial crisis, by 2015 had converged to the level of private companies, real GDP in 2015 would have been 13 to 15 percent larger. Achieving this hypothetical endpoint would have required annual growth between 2007 and 2015 to have been as much as 2 percentage points more than the recorded pace of 8.6 percent. This opportunity still exists. Going forward, if the performance of state firms over time approaches that of private firms and/or the underperforming assets of state firms are acquired by more productive private firms, China's growth would gain substantially. In addition, borrowing by state firms to cover their financial losses would moderate, and risks in the financial system would be systematically reduced. In short, on the assumption that the rising trade frictions between China and the United States are relatively short-lived, China's potential growth for a considerable period into the future is more rapid than the 6 to 7 percent rate observed in recent years.

Chapter 3 analyzes the current efforts to reform underperforming state-owned firms. Elements of this approach include corporatization, the conversion of traditional state-owned companies into limited liability companies; top-down mergers of the largest state companies overseen by state bureaucrats and party functionaries rather than business-oriented managers; mixed ownership, the introduction of private capital into state companies; debt-to-equity swaps that would salvage state companies by reducing their indebtedness; and governance reforms that would make most state companies responsible for their profits and losses. But the state has pursued the first three reform components for a decade or more, the period in which the return on state assets has plummeted. And the latter two components have not gotten off the ground. A new approach is needed.

What specific reforms must China undertake to capture the higher potential growth analyzed in chapter 2? Chapter 4 focuses on reducing the barriers to entry for more productive private firms, particularly in services such as banking and logistics. China should also encourage more bottom-up, market-oriented merger and acquisition activity allowing private firms to take over underperforming state assets. Reform must force into bankruptcy more long-lived zombie firms (僵尸企业), mostly state-owned, that now survive by borrowing ever increasing amounts from state-owned banks. The takeover of failing Dongbei Steel by China's most successful private steel entrepreneur is a good, but unfortunately isolated, precedent.

Another important reform discussed in this chapter would take place in the financial sector, by encouraging a more efficient and market-oriented allocation of funds by banks and capital markets. China also needs to upgrade the use of financial metrics in evaluating the performance of state companies.

The concluding chapter notes the various political economy constraints to adopting a more far-reaching reform program and the implications for the global economy. At the most fundamental level, President Xi fears that downsizing state enterprises could slow economic growth. More important, he and his allies in the leadership councils of China no doubt fear that reforms could trigger social unrest, unemployment, financial instability, and loss of support among crucial vested interests—particularly local party and government officials and top managers in China's state-owned enterprises. Pursuing a more reform-oriented course faces undeniable challenges. But perhaps the main one relates to President Xi's own view of himself as the commander in chief of the Chinese economic state. On the other hand, President Xi may recognize that his desire to raise living standards and promote further globalization will probably depend on a more ambitious domestic economic reform program. Which course he chooses will powerfully affect the future not only of the Chinese economy but also of the global economy.

1

Understanding China's Economic Slowdown after the Global Financial Crisis

The Chinese economy is so immense, and its connection to the economies of the rest of the world so entangled, that it is sometimes perceived more as a source of danger than as a contributor to global prosperity. From one perspective, the supposed threat emanates from China's slowing growth and buildup of domestic debt since the global financial crisis, creating a fear that these debt burdens could trigger a major financial crisis and drag down the global economy, which has become increasingly dependent on China as a locomotive of economic expansion. The underlying assumption of these anxieties, of course, is that the world needs China to continue its steady growth as a force for global economic health.

Ironically, from another perspective, a profound danger emanates from China's inexorable growth: the widespread concern that China's economic progress will embolden its political ambitions, threatening the security interests of the United States and its allies in Asia. These anxieties rest on the assumption that China will soon overtake the United States as the world's largest economy measured by exchange rates. The fears focus on China's aggressive industrial policies such as Made in China 2025, which could enable China to attain global dominance of artificial intelligence and other advanced technologies that are seen as the foundation of future economic growth. The Critics advocate tightened disclosure requirements for state-led acquisitions of foreign firms and more comprehensive national security screening to restrict access of Chinese firms to advanced technology in high-income economies (Wübbeke et al. 2016, 61–65). In the United States, the Foreign Investment

Risk Review Modernization Act and the Export Control Reform Act came into effect in August 2018. The former is designed to strengthen existing regulations against foreign investment that might put national security at risk and the latter authorizes the US Commerce Department to update controls on technology leakage through exports (Chorzempa 2018).

In short, there are two fears, based in polar opposite expectations of China's future growth performance. The first sees danger from the adverse effects of China's possibly slowing growth; the second sees danger from China's continuing rise. The evidence cited in this book provides a more balanced assessment of China's medium-run growth potential and the composition of that growth, to provide an analytical basis for understanding whether one or both concerns are misplaced and the implications of China's growth for the global economy over the medium term.

China's Global Economic Role

In the decade prior to the global financial crisis China grew at an average rate of a little over 10 percent, in the process becoming the world's second largest economy, measured at market exchange rates. Its contribution to global economic growth was way more than the contribution of either the United States or the euro area. Since 2010, however, the pace of China's expansion has slowed, to under 7 percent in 2015, 2016, and 2017. Growth of only 6.7 percent in 2016 was the slowest pace in a quarter century (National Bureau of Statistics of China 2017a). Still, China in 2015 accounted for about one-third of global growth, an even larger share than in 2010 when it last achieved double-digit growth (IMF 2016a, 17), primarily because global growth had not recovered to its precrisis pace and because China's economy in 2015 was half again as large as in 2010. Its share of global growth in both 2016 and 2017 was similarly large. This is a remarkable role for an economy that accounts for only 15 percent of global GDP (Guo 2017b; National Bureau of Statistics of China, Comprehensive Office 2018).[1]

Despite its outsized positive contribution to global growth in recent years, in some periods since the global financial crisis, notably in the summer of 2015 and again in early 2016, gyrations in China's domestic stock market and uncertainty surrounding its exchange rate policy have made China a source of global financial market instability. These concerns emerged again, though less intensely, in 2018 when China's stock market and currency both weakened, at least partially in response to the fear that trade frictions between China and

---

1. Based on market exchange rates, China's share of global GDP expanded from 12.5 percent in 2013 to 15.3 percent in 2017.

the United States would slow China's growth. The correlation between the movement of asset prices and exchange rates in China and other countries has increased since 2015 and likely will strengthen further if China ultimately succeeds in further liberalizing its capital account (IMF 2016b, 179–81).

In addition, influential voices argue that China confronts numerous obstacles to sustaining growth over the medium term at even a much more modest pace than in recent years. These obstacles include potential political instability, weak governance indicators such as the rule of law and voice and accountability, and severe economic imbalances, including excessive reliance on investment, unsustainably fast growth of credit, and domestic savings that are far too large to be absorbed productively at home (Wolf 2016). Lant Pritchett and Larry Summers (2014) are more explicit, arguing that China is long overdue for an economic correction that would bring its growth rate more in line with the median global historic rate of 2 percent per capita. They challenge the view that they label Asiaphoria, the vision that continued rapid growth of China and India will shift the global economic center of gravity even more decisively to Asia.

The latter scenario would severely limit global economic growth, far beyond the transmission of financial market instability observed in mid-2015 and early 2016. China has become deeply integrated in global value chains and is a top ten export market for over 100 countries accounting for about 80 percent of world GDP (IMF 2016b, 171). Australia's large exports of iron ore, for example, go overwhelmingly to China and Chile sends a large share of its copper exports there. So the shock to the rest of the world resulting from a Chinese hard landing would be transmitted primarily by a drop in China's imports. The IMF, for example, estimates that a 1 percentage point negative shock to China's final demand growth would reduce global GDP growth of 0.25 percent after one year. Thus, the rapid slowing of China's growth by 4.65 percentage points, as postulated by Pritchett and Summers (2014), would reduce global GDP growth by more than a percentage point (IMF 2016b, 174).[2] Slower Chinese growth would inflict even greater economic damage on Asian countries more closely linked to China through global supply chains (World Bank 2016, 103). A study by the World Bank and a number of other organizations estimates that as much as 60 to 70 percent of global trade involves global production networks, parts, components, and semifinished goods that

---

2. As discussed later in this chapter, Pritchett and Summers (2014) offer several alternative estimates of China's growth in the two-decade period 2013–33. One is based on their observation that the average growth deceleration after a period of super rapid economic growth in other countries was 4.65 percentage points.

cross international borders, sometimes many times, before they are assembled as final goods. China is the best example among a small number of developing countries that are deeply involved in these global value chains (World Bank et al. 2017, 1–2)

Even if China's growth remains relatively strong over the medium term, say 5 percent or more, and if this is achieved by a further rebalancing of the sources of growth—a smaller role for investment and a larger role for consumption—there would be important consequences for other economies, both beneficial and damaging. Already by the middle of the 2010s, China's overall slowdown and initial shifting away from investment and exports and toward internal domestic consumption had helped moderate global commodity prices, particularly for nonfuel commodities (IMF 2016b, 178). Should this rebalancing continue (other factors remaining unchanged), these prices could decline further, squeezing commodity exporters, such as Australia, Brazil, and Chile. On the other hand commodity importers, including the United States, would benefit from paying less for these commodities. Since investment in China is more import intensive than consumption, additional rebalancing of the sources of China's growth away from investment would probably hurt major suppliers of machinery and equipment and other investment goods (IMF 2016b, 175). Asian countries, except New Zealand, are more exposed to China's investment than they are to its consumption, so even a rebalancing that left China's growth unchanged would slow the growth of exports of these countries to China, impeding their growth prospects (IMF 2016d, 53).

Causes of the Slowdown

China's growth slowed after the global financial crisis because of several factors, but there is no question that the decline was significant: from an average of 12 percent in 2005–08, prior to the global financial crisis, to an average of just under 7 percent in 2015–16 (National Bureau of Statistics of China 2016a, 24). Moreover, achieving even this greatly reduced pace of economic expansion required a massive increase in credit and a significant step up in the share of output devoted to investment. The decline in the efficiency of resource use implicit in these trends was also evident in a sharp drop in total factor productivity. Wu (2017, 17) estimates that total factor productivity declined by 2.1 percent per year in 2007–12, compared with annual gains of 1.2, 1.6, and 1.2 percent in 1980–91, 1991–2001, and 2001–07, respectively.[3]

---

3. The numbers cited are Wu's estimates of what he labels aggregate total factor productivity growth. His alternative Domar-weighted calculation generates somewhat slower total factor

Table 1.1 Factors affecting China's growth

Number	Factor	Effect on growth post–global financial crisis to 2016	Effect on potential growth, 2016–
1	Above potential growth before the global financial crisis	Negative	Neutral
2	Weak global recovery	Negative	Neutral
3	Infrastructure and housing investment	Positive	Neutral
4	Pace of reform	Negative	Potentially positive
5	Rising debt burden	Neutral	Negative
6	Demography Changing sectoral composition Shrinking labor force	 Neutral Slightly negative	 Neutral Slightly negative
7	Reversion to mean	Negative	Negative

This chapter examines seven contributors to China's economic slowdown and the simultaneous decline in total factor productivity since the global financial crisis. Some factors appear to be transitory, i.e., the product of specific circumstances that may not endure. If these transitory factors fade away, China's growth could strengthen slightly from its current pace of around 6 to 7 percent. Other factors are likely to persist and perhaps even strengthen, suggesting that China's potential growth is likely to be below its current pace. The first group of explanations of the slowdown is more positive for global economic growth, the second group obviously more negative. Table 1.1 provides a summary assessment of the effects of the seven factors on both growth since the global financial crisis and potential growth.

Above Potential Growth Prior to the Global Financial Crisis

The first of the transitory factors contributing to China's slowdown, one that is frequently overlooked, is that prior to the global financial crisis China was growing above its medium-term potential rate, largely because a rising domestic saving-investment imbalance and a depreciating currency rapidly expanded the surplus in its goods and services trade with the rest of the world. This

---

productivity growth in 1980–2007, but the same −2.1 percent per annum for the most recent period. Wu's estimates of total factor productivity in China prior to the global financial crisis are substantially below the estimate of Perkins and Rawski (2008), cited later in this study, primarily because his estimates are based on an aggregate production possibility frontier framework, rather than the usual aggregate production function approach. I prefer the Perkins and Rawski methodology, but their estimates cover only through 2005 while Wu's estimates cover through 2012.

external surplus, which along with consumption and investment contributes to growth, more than doubled to 5.4 percent of GDP in 2005 compared with the prior year and then expanded further to reach a peak of 8.7 percent in 2007, an all-time record for any large trading economy. Although the surplus moderated slightly in 2008, on average in the four years 2005–08 the trade surplus added 1.3 percentage points to China's economic growth (National Bureau of Statistics of China 2016a, 37–38).

China's exchange rate policy and macroeconomic developments drove these external surpluses. Beginning in the mid-1990s the authorities pegged the Chinese currency to the US dollar. The dollar appreciated from the mid-1990s through early 2002. Although the peg meant that the exchange rate of the renminbi vis-à-vis the dollar was unchanged, dollar appreciation led to a significant appreciation of the Chinese currency on a real effective basis, a measure that takes into account the value of the renminbi against the currencies of all of China's major trading partners, including the US dollar.[4] But China's trade surplus over this period was relatively small and stable. Usually currency appreciation would make a country's goods less competitive on global markets and imports into its domestic market more competitive, thus typically reducing an existing trade surplus or generating a larger trade deficit. This did not happen in the case of China, suggesting that productivity gains in the tradable sector, which lowered the domestic prices of both export goods and goods that compete with imports, roughly offset the real appreciation of the Chinese currency.

But starting in early 2002 the US dollar gradually depreciated. Given the continued peg of the yuan to the dollar, the exchange rate of the renminbi vis-à-vis the dollar was unchanged, but dollar depreciation caused the exchange rate of the renminbi to depreciate, again on a real effective basis. The combination of this depreciation and continued productivity improvements in the tradable sector led to a rapidly rising Chinese trade and current account surplus.

Thus, beginning in 2001, China's central bank had to begin purchasing foreign exchange to maintain the peg of the renminbi to the US dollar. In the absence of official exchange market intervention, the currency of a country with a trade surplus would tend to automatically appreciate. The supply of foreign currency in the exchange market would exceed the demand, causing the foreign currency to fall in value and the domestic currency to appreciate. But in China central bank purchases of foreign exchange cut off this adjustment mechanism. These purchases started modestly in 2001–02 but quickly

---

4. The measure also considers inflation in China relative to its major trading partners.

rose to average almost 10 percent of GDP in 2004–06 and then peaked at 14 percent of GDP in 2007 (Goldstein and Lardy 2009, 21). The combination of the renminbi's peg to the US dollar and central bank intervention in the foreign exchange market resulted in an undervaluation of the renminbi, which pushed China's trade surplus to its record high share of GDP in 2007. The massive intervention by the central bank in the foreign exchange market to prevent the appreciation of the currency and the resulting unprecedented external surplus are the basis for the assessment that China engaged in currency manipulation (Goldstein and Lardy 2009).

From a macroeconomic perspective, the rising external surplus reflected a rise in national savings relative to investment. The share of national income devoted to investment was largely unchanged in 2005–08 but the national saving rate rose over the same period, largely because of a sharp increase in household savings.

China's saving-investment imbalance and its undervalued currency, in turn, both distorted the allocation of domestic resources among the various economic activities and led to widespread international criticism of its exchange rate policy. Thus, continuing trade's outsized contribution to economic growth was not sustainable, either economically or politically.

Starting in mid-2005 the authorities allowed the exchange rate to slowly appreciate and after 2008 China's saving-investment imbalance and trade surplus both gradually fell, the latter reaching only 2.2 percent of GDP by 2016, in the process reducing economic growth by an average of 0.8 percentage point in 2009–16 (State Administration of Foreign Exchange International Balance of Payments Analysis Small Group 2017, 17; National Bureau of Statistics of China 2017e, 79). Thus, moving from a growing and unsustainably high trade surplus in 2005–08 to a surplus in 2009–16 that was falling to a more sustainable level reduced China's growth by 2.1 percentage points, accounting for about half of China's growth slowdown since the global financial crisis.[5]

Weak Recovery of Global Economic and Trade Growth after the Global Financial Crisis

A second potential contributor to the slowdown in China's growth, at least through 2016, was the weak global recovery from the global financial crisis. The pace of global GDP growth, especially in developed countries, was slower than precrisis growth, and global trade recovered very slowly: Global mer-

---

5. GDP growth in 2009–16 averaged 8.2 percent, 3.8 percentage points less than the average 12 percent pace recorded in 2005–08.

chandise trade volume expanded at only 2.6 and 1.3 percent in 2015 and 2016, respectively, well below the average annual 4.7 percent rate since 1980. Part of the trade slowdown, of course, reflects the slower growth of the global economy. But the ratio of world merchandise trade growth to world GDP growth also declined sharply. In the five years through 2016 this ratio was slightly less than 1, a clear break from the 1990s when merchandise trade grew at twice the pace of global GDP growth (WTO 2017, 18).

China was not immune to the weakening global economic environment. Indeed, slowing global trade reinforced the decline in China's net exports caused by the strengthening of the renminbi and the moderation in the saving-investment imbalance. In value terms measured in domestic currency China's exports more than tripled between 2003 and 2008. The cumulative expansion in 2010 through 2015 was only 44 percent (National Bureau of Statistics of China 2016a, 99). Accordingly, China's share of global exports peaked in 2015 before falling in 2016–17 for the first time in decades.[6]

Moreover, the slow pace of global growth also contributed to declining total factor productivity after the global financial crisis. For both China and emerging markets more generally in the short run there is a strong correlation between export growth and the growth of total factor productivity. Normally exports are the most volatile component of aggregate demand in emerging economies. Strongly rising exports increase employment and income, as underutilized capital comes on stream. This combination increases total factor productivity. When exports are weak or falling, demand and employment weaken against a fixed capital stock and thus total factor productivity growth slows or even falls (Anderson 2016). According to Anderson, when global trade growth improves, both productivity growth and GDP growth strengthen in emerging markets, including China.

Thus, part of the decline in total factor productivity in China since the global financial crisis is due to the slowing of its export growth.

Note that the contribution of slowing global trade to China's economic slowdown and declining total factor productivity probably is also transitory, as the IMF (2017c, 14) forecasts that the ratio of global trade expansion to global growth in 2017 will rise to 1.4, reversing the 2011–16 pattern when the ratio was less than 1. China benefited from this trend in 2017 as its goods and services surplus contributed 9 percent of China's growth (i.e., 0.63 percentage points of 6.9 percent GDP growth), the largest contribution of trade to growth since 2007 (National Bureau of Statistics of China 2018b).

---

6. "China's share of global and Asian exports is falling," *Economist*, March 8, 2018, www.economist.com (accessed on May 3, 2018).

Rising Infrastructure and Housing Investment

The rapid growth of investment in real estate and infrastructure undoubtedly contributed to China's growth in the early stages of the global financial crisis but probably also contributed to the decline in both total factor productivity and some financial metrics. The contribution of housing, which accounts for the largest share of real estate investment, to the growth of GDP is understated in China's national accounts (Lardy 2012, 157–61). This understatement of growth underestimates total factor productivity, i.e., output per combined inputs of capital and labor. Similarly, the financial payoff from infrastructure investment, which creates very long-lived assets, typically occurs with a lag. The increase in infrastructure investment in China was large during the global financial crisis, but because of the lag official data on return on assets may overstate the decline in the efficiency of investment compared with precrisis years.

High-speed passenger rail is a good example of long-lived infrastructure investment that will generate returns for generations. High-speed rail also has important network effects, i.e., the gains are not entirely captured until the network is more fully developed, allowing increasing amounts of freight to move onto the preexisting rail system and move continuously over longer distances as a larger share of passenger traffic is carried on the dedicated high-speed rail network. The World Bank anticipated that additional freight revenues would largely cover the capital costs of the high-speed rail network (Lardy 2012, 28–31). In the early years of the development of China's high-speed rail network, revenues were modest and returns on large initial capital outlays inevitably were very low. But as the network was built out, reaching 23,000 kilometers by 2016, annual passenger traffic exploded to well over 1 billion, accounting for more than 40 percent of all railway passenger traffic (National Bureau of Statistics of China 2017e, 540). On the heavily traveled Beijing-Shanghai route, average daily passenger traffic on high-speed trains jumped from 132,000 to 505,000 between 2011 and mid-2017. Most of the increase in passenger traffic on this route has been accommodated by reducing the intervals between trains to three minutes during peak periods, making more efficient use of the high-speed rail network.[7] Operating profits as a result

---

7. Zhao Lei, "New trains ease pressure off busy Beijing-Shanghai high-speed rail," *China Daily*, June 25, 2017, www.chinadaily.com (accessed on November 13, 2017); "The Beijing-Shanghai high-speed rail has overcome obstacles, operating for five years and conveying more than 450 million passengers," National Rail Administration, July 1, 2016, www.nra.gov.cn (accessed on November 13, 2017); "The Beijing-Shanghai high-speed rail has operated safely for six years; carrying more than 630 million passengers," July 1, 2017, http://travel.news.cn (accessed on November 13, 2017).

have improved. The Beijing-Shanghai line lost RMB3.7 billion in 2012, its first full year of operation; it turned profitable in 2014 and earned profits of RMB6.66 billion in 2015.[8] A similar pattern may emerge on other high-speed rail routes, all of which were making losses through 2015. The leading candidate for an early turn to profitability is the heavily traveled Guangzhou-Wuhan line. Interest payments on the large debt of the China Railway Corporation have exceeded the company's operating profits since at least 2015. But the most recent World Bank analysis is that given the long life of the high-speed rail system, which distributes the fixed costs over a period of decades, the system should be able to cover its costs on a long-term basis.[9]

The contribution of this factor to China's declining factor productivity and weakening financial metrics should be largely transitory. The annual growth of real estate investment moderated from a peak of 31 percent in 2010 to a low of only 2 percent in 2015, before recovering slightly to a more sustainable level averaging 7 percent in 2016–17 (National Bureau of Statistics of China 2018b; 2017e, 309). Similarly, the growth of investment in infrastructure moderated after 2010.[10] As a result, the degree of understatement of GDP and the exaggerated weakness in some financial metrics should dissipate.

Slowing Pace of Economic Reform and Resurgence of the State

A fourth factor contributing to China's slowdown, one emphasized in this book, is the slowing pace of economic reform, reflected in the growing role of the state in resource allocation and deteriorating financial performance of state companies. China's last big push on reform of state-owned enterprises came under the leadership of Premier Zhu Rongji, who led both a major downsizing and restructuring of state companies starting in 1997–98 and a significant opening of the economy to external competition, paving the way for

---

8. "The Beijing-Shanghai high-speed rail earned RMB6.5 billion last year, the only profitable high-speed rail line in China," *Xinhua News*, July 20, 2016, http://news.xinhuanet.com/politics (accessed on November 14, 2017).

9. Tom Mitchell and Xinning Liu, "China's high-speed rail network signals rapid expansion of debt," *Financial Times*, August 15, 2018, 3. This positive assessment is conditional on ticket prices of the high-speed rail system rising in line with inflation.

10. Official data on infrastructure investment are measured according to the concept of fixed asset investment, which, as explained in footnote 12 in this chapter, overstates capital investment in infrastructure. The analysis in the text is based on the assumption that annual infrastructure investment as a share of annual total fixed asset investment is a good proxy for the share of annual capital investment devoted to infrastructure. These annual shares are then multiplied by annual data on capital formation as a share of GDP to develop an annual series of estimated infrastructure investment as a share of GDP.

China's entry into the World Trade Organization (WTO) in 2001. As shown in chapter 2, this combination of reforms enhanced the role of the market, increasing competition and thus the return on assets of state firms, which boosted China's economic growth.

The subsequent decade-long administration of President Hu Jintao and Premier Wen Jiabao beginning in 2003 had much more modest economic reform ambitions, probably in part because China's economic performance during the first five years of their leadership was extremely strong, largely due to the market-oriented reforms of the Zhu Rongji era and the policies that led to an undervaluation of the renminbi, which pushed growth above its medium-term potential. Moreover, under President Hu China began turning away from the opening up policy of the Zhu era. In 2006 the government published the Medium-Term Plan for Science and Technology, which had a statist orientation, and in December 2007 the Ministry of Finance issued a policy on "indigenous innovation" restricting government purchase of certain products to those developed by domestic enterprises. Several circulars were later issued by government agencies spelling out in detail the new "buy China" policy (USTR 2011, 87–88). This explicit import substitution initiative was a marked departure from previous policy.

Moreover, the response of the Hu-Wen leadership to the global financial crisis was not a renewed effort at economic reform but rather a massive credit-financed stimulus program, which maintained growth at close to double digits in 2008–11. But subsequently, even though the ratio of credit outstanding to GDP continued to rise, growth slowed persistently through 2016. As argued in chapter 2, weakening economic performance of state companies was a major contributor to this slowdown. The Hu-Wen leadership did not respond with more reforms, choosing instead to run out the clock, probably on the calculation that the reforms necessary to boost growth would be disruptive in the short run and probably not improve economic performance in their remaining time in office.

But slowing growth in the face of rapidly expanding credit seemed to be a wake-up call for China's next leadership. In the fall of 2013, about a year after Xi Jinping became the general secretary of the Chinese Communist Party and a little more than six months after he assumed the office of president, the Third Plenum of the 18th Chinese Communist Party Congress endorsed a far-reaching blueprint for economic reform. It is easy to get lost in the details, but the signal phrase it contained, "We must ensure that the market has a decisive role in the allocation of resources," had never appeared in an official document of the Chinese Communist Party (Chinese Communist Party Central Committee 2013). Less noticed at the time, perhaps because similar language had appeared in many earlier party and government documents, was the call for "unswervingly consolidating and developing the public economy, persisting in the dominant position of public ownership, giving full play to the leading role of the state sector, continuously increasing its vitality, controlling force and influence."

Indeed, under the leadership of President Xi, state industrial policy increasingly displaced the market-oriented economic reform program advanced in the Third Plenum document. China in effect doubled down on the indigenous innovation initiative launched under President Hu. In May 2015 China's State Council launched the Made in China 2025 program, which called for breakthroughs in ten priority industries, including advanced information technology, robotics, new energy vehicles, new materials, pharmaceuticals, and advanced medical devices (State Council 2015a). The 13th Five-Year Plan (2016–20), approved the next year by the National People's Congress, advanced more detailed objectives for six industry subsectors, including many in high-tech manufacturing (National Development and Reform Commission 2016). While the plan encouraged further opening up of the economy to private firms, the tide was turning in favor of state firms. The following year the highest administrative level of the government called for consolidating and strengthening a group of central state-owned enterprises, meaning that the state should exercise sole or absolute (i.e., greater than 50 percent) control of firms in many industries and sectors (State Council 2016a). Chairman Xi authoritatively reiterated this theme in his lengthy speech to the 19th Party Congress in October 2017, when he stated, "We will support state capital in becoming stronger, doing better, and growing bigger" (Xi 2017).

Rather than pushing the Third Plenum reforms, President Xi in his first five-year term focused on his signature anticorruption campaign; consolidated his own personal political power in the run-up to the 19th Party Congress in the fall of 2017; amended the constitution to eliminate the two-term limit on the offices of president and vice president at the 13th National People's Congress in the spring of 2018; enhanced the role of the Chinese Communist Party; exerted tighter control over the internet; and emphasized state-owned enterprises as a major source of economic growth. These policies were pursued despite accumulating evidence showing a systematic decline in the economic performance of state-owned firms and slowing investment by more productive private firms. (Chapter 2 analyzes the declining performance of state firms in detail.) Thus, early optimism that the party's Third Plenum document signaled a renewed commitment to further market-oriented reform ultimately gave way to the assessment that President Xi had little interest in "pushing through a complex and broadly market-oriented economic reform program,"

Figure 1.1   State and private investment, 2006–16

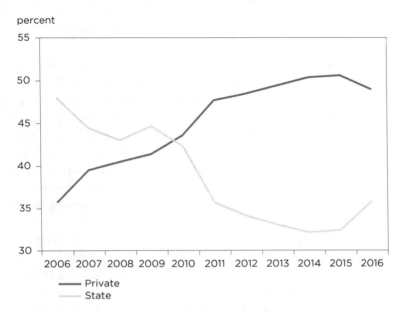

percent

Sources: National Bureau of Statistics of China (2017e, 310–11); National Bureau of Statistics of China, data.stats.gov.cn (accessed on September 5, 2017).

preferring instead "to build a bigger and more powerful state sector" (Kroeber 2016).

One important indicator of the enhanced role of state firms and the state more generally after Xi assumed office is the deceleration of private investment relative to state investment starting in 2012 (figure 1.1). The share of private investment in total investment showed a clear and sustained rapid rise, from 36 percent in 2006 (when this time series begins) to 48 percent in 2011. In this interval, private investment expanded at a pace equal to 2.6 times that of state investment.[11] As a result, the share of state investment fell from 48 to

---

11. Throughout this study data on state investment include investment by traditional state-owned enterprises and by state enterprises that have been corporatized (becoming limited liability companies or shareholding limited companies) in which the state is in control because it is the sole, majority, or dominant owner. In addition, all 50:50 joint ventures between state companies and foreign firms are considered to be state-controlled. The coverage of investment by private companies is similarly broad, including investment by registered private companies as well as investment by shareholding companies in which the sole, majority, or dominant owner is private. For details, see Lardy (2016, 38).

36 percent—the mirror image of the changed share of private investment.[12] Economic liberalization had opened more sectors to private investment and increased private firms' access to both bank loans and the domestic equity market (Lardy 2014).

But starting in 2012 through 2015 the pace of private investment slowed markedly, to only 1.3 times that of state investment, and in 2016 fell well below that of state investment. Several factors appear to underlie this change. First, by 2014 private firms already accounted for over three-quarters of investment in manufacturing. But, as outlined later in this chapter, when the service sector began to displace industry as the major source of growth starting in 2013, the growth of both manufacturing output and investment in manufacturing moderated, inevitably slowing the pace of private investment, which was concentrated in manufacturing. Second, the pace of opening the service sector to private investment slowed, reducing the potential growth of private investment. Third, in a stark reversal of the earlier trend, beginning in 2012 banks directed a larger share of credit to state firms, essentially crowding out private investment. Finally, starting in 2015, the increased role of both the state and the party in the economy and the illegal seizure of private enterprises by the state chilled the investment enthusiasm of private entrepreneurs. In speeches at the 19th Party Congress in the fall of 2017 and at the National People's Congress in the spring of 2018 President Xi called for an expanded role of the party, including enhancing the role of party committees, even in private enterprises. At the Third Plenum of the 19th Party Congress in March 2018, the central committee adopted a plan calling on "the party to exercise leadership over all areas of endeavor in every part of the country" (Chinese

---

12. This analysis relies on data on fixed asset investment, the only Chinese published data on investment that are disaggregated by ownership. However, fixed asset investment data are flawed for at least two reasons. First, they include the value of purchases of land, existing buildings, and second-hand equipment, transactions that only change ownership of assets and do not add to productive capacity. Second, local officials tend to exaggerate the data. Moreover, the degree of overstatement has increased substantially over time; by 2016 the value of fixed asset investment was 90 percent larger than gross fixed capital formation, which is based on the national income accounts and is considered the best measure of investment (National Bureau of Statistics of China 2017e, 74, 294). Thus, the validity of the analysis in the text depends on the implicit assumption that the degree of exaggeration is similar across ownership categories. In 2018 the statistical authorities began to revise the compilation of fixed asset investment data to reduce the degree of overstatement of capital formation. They began this process focusing on larger investment projects, typically undertaken by state companies. This revision predictably led to a substantial decline in the reported pace of investment by state companies relative to private companies. Thus, the assumption that the degree of exaggeration of the data is similar across ownership categories appears to be no longer valid.

Communist Party Central Committee 2018). This plan too is likely to further erode the confidence of private businesses.

The resumption of state-led growth, in which a growing share of resources is flowing into investment by relatively low productivity state firms, and an increasingly omnipresent party are contributing to China's growth slowdown. The fast growth of investment by more productive private firms before, which was boosting China's growth, has now moderated due to a combination of political factors and "crowding out," inevitably slowing China's growth.

Whether this change is transitory or persistent will depend on policy. If President Xi embraces economic reform in his second five-year term (2018–23), along the lines endorsed by the Chinese Communist Party in the fall of 2013, it will be transitory. If the role of the market expands, particularly if the allocation of capital becomes more responsive to rates of return, and the property rights of private businesses are assured, the private sector likely will resume making an outsized contribution to economic growth. The difficulty the regime faces in guaranteeing property rights was reflected in the response of Premier Li Keqiang to a query on the slowing pace of private investment at his press conference marking the closing of the National People's Congress in March 2018. He acknowledged that private investment was weak and explained that it was due to "weak protection of property rights and some other factors."[13] This response suggests that a previous joint call of the Chinese Communist Party Central Committee and State Council (2016) to improve the protection of property rights had fallen short. That document candidly acknowledged that the state had illegally seized and frozen the property of private entrepreneurs. On the other hand, if President Xi continues to emphasize that the Chinese Communist Party must control all aspects of China and pursue policies that favor state firms and hinder the more productive private sector, private investment will remain weak, leading one to expect a further deterioration in the pace of growth over the medium term.

Rising Burden of China's Debt

A fifth contributor to slowing growth, which is clearly persistent and thus may have important implications for China's potential growth, is a blend of the rising burden of domestic debt and the difficulty of rebalancing the sources of growth, views most closely associated with Michael Pettis. He has long argued that China's expansion had become structurally dependent on an unsustainable increase in debt and that its growth would soon slow by 1 to 1.5 percent-

---

13. "Premier Li Keqiang meets the media after the NPC's annual session closes," *China Daily*, March 21, 2018, 6.

age points annually and as a result growth in 2012–22 "will average 3-4% at best" (Pettis 2016b). He correctly notes that credit has been growing more rapidly than GDP since the global financial crisis and believes that the resulting rise in the ratio of domestic debt to GDP increasingly constrains economic growth. He argues quite sensibly that in the long run China must reach the point where its debt servicing costs rise in line with debt servicing capacity. The latter, he believes, is no more than, and likely somewhat less than, the growth of GDP.

If debt is not paid down, Pettis anticipates that the debt constraint will reduce growth to less than half current levels. Given state ownership of most of the assets in the banking system, he does not anticipate a financial crisis. But he believes that China would be able to grow its way out of the debt burden only through either a massive increase in total factor productivity or a rapid transition to a growth model that relies primarily on private consumption expenditure, rather than exports and investment, as the primary source of demand. He argues that the former is unattainable and the latter would be possible only if the government transfers income equivalent to 1 to 4 percentage points of GDP to households annually to accelerate the growth of private consumption expenditure. Such transfers would decrease the share of output devoted to investment, thereby avoiding an unsustainable further increase in domestic debt but necessarily reducing China's growth to between 3 and 4 percent annually (Pettis 2016a).

Pettis doubts the government will make the transfers necessary to boost consumption, so he anticipates that the rising burden of debt will lead to "a long, drawn-out grinding away of debt, with growth slowly dropping to very low levels" (Pettis 2017). The mechanism Pettis has in mind is that with debt servicing capacity growing more slowly than debt servicing costs, the debt burden "can rise until credit growth can no longer be forced up to the point where it can be used to roll over existing debt with enough margin fully to fund as much new economic activity that Beijing targets" (Pettis 2016c). The Pettis thesis is evaluated later in this chapter. To preview, he underestimates the progress China has made so far in rebalancing the sources of growth. Household income is already growing annually by close to 1 percentage point of GDP, without the direct government transfers that Pettis judges essential for rebalancing progress. And, as shown in chapter 2, China's problem is not so much a high aggregate level of domestic debt but the misallocation of credit to a subset of least efficient, loss-making state firms.

Demography as Destiny

A sixth potential contributor to China's slowing growth, clearly persistent, argues that the changing sectoral composition of the workforce and demographic factors already have begun to slow China's growth and will become more of a drag in coming years. The movement of workers from agriculture, where output per worker was very low, to urban jobs, where output per worker was much higher, was a major contributor to China's economic growth after economic reform began in the late 1970s, when the state, at least at the margin, started easing onerous restrictions on rural-urban migration. Output per worker in agriculture in 1978 was only about one-sixth that in nonagriculture. Given the huge gap in output per worker between the two sectors, the reallocation of labor out of agriculture accounted for about half of all growth in the first decade of reform (Brandt, Hsieh, and Zhu 2008, 690, 696–97). But once the surplus labor in agriculture has been absorbed, frequently called the Lewis turning point, this major source of growth disappears. Couldn't this factor have contributed to the slowdown in China's growth over the past decade?

Moreover, a more purely demographic factor may impede China's growth going forward. Fertility in China began to decline in the mid-1960s. The formal introduction of the one-child policy in 1980 reinforced the decline, creating a demographic dividend in the form of "rapid drops in youth dependency, and a corresponding increase in the growth of the labour force relative to that of the total population, and hence in the working-age to non-working age population ratio." This demographic dividend accounted for between one-sixth and one-quarter of per capita GDP growth between 1980 and 2010 (Golley, Tyers, and Zhou 2016, 243).

However, the ratio of the working age to non–working age population peaked in 2010 and is now declining and China's population is beginning to age. Moreover, since China's labor force participation rate is already relatively high, exceeding that of the United States, there is not much leeway to offset this demographic drag by raising the labor force participation rate.

It is not clear that changes in the sectoral composition of the workforce or demographic factors explain China's slowdown since the global financial crisis or will have a decisive effect on China's potential growth. First, the contribution of labor reallocation from agriculture to nonagriculture to GDP growth "occurred mainly near the start of China's reform process" (Brandt, Hsieh, and Zhu 2008, 696). In the next 16 years of reform, from 1988 through 2004, this reallocation accounted for only about a tenth of all growth.

Second, wage data also support the view that the Lewis turning point, when the surplus labor in agriculture has been largely absorbed and urban wages are no longer held down by the so-called unlimited supply of rural labor, occurred two decades ago, not since the global financial crisis. Garnaut and Huang (2006) observed that real wages started rising in the late 1990s and remained high through the middle of the next decade, suggesting that the Lewis turning point had already passed and that the stimulus to growth from low-cost labor was waning. In short, neither the productivity analysis nor the trends in wages support the hypothesis that the exhaustion of surplus labor contributed to the slowdown in China's growth since the global financial crisis. This factor began weighing on China's growth starting in the late 1990s.

Looking ahead, what is the potential drag on growth from the shrinking working age population, a factor that has come into play since the global financial crisis? Perhaps much less than is sometimes assumed. Throughout the reform period the growth of labor productivity, i.e., output per worker, has been a far more important contributor to China's growth than the expanding size of the labor force. In 1978–2005, China's raw labor force expansion accounted for less than 10 percent of China's growth. Indeed, improvements in the quality of labor, as measured by increased educational attainment, were a more important contributor to growth than the simple expansion of the size of the workforce (Perkins and Rawski 2008, 839).

Moreover, in the coming two or more decades, two factors could potentially offset the shrinking size of China's working age population. The first, already suggested, is greater investment in human capital, which raises worker productivity. In 2005 the average worker in China had only a junior high school education (Perkins and Rawski 2008, 838). While educational attainment improved over the next decade, by 2015 less than 30 percent of the Chinese workforce had a high school education (Li et al. 2017, 27). This is well below the level of educational attainment in some other upper-middle-income countries—for example, Mexico (46 percent), South Africa (42 percent), and Malaysia (51 percent)—and far below the level in a few lower-middle-income countries, such as the Philippines (58 percent). China predictably lags the OECD average of 80 percent by an even larger margin (Li et al. 2017, 35–36). Thus, China has considerable potential to enhance productivity by improving the quality of labor.

A second potential offset is later retirement. When the Chinese Communist Party came to power in 1949 life expectancy in China was only 35 years, and in the early 1950s the government set the statutory retirement ages at 60 for men and 55 for women (State Council Information Office 2017). Although average life expectancy in China more than doubled to 76 years by

2014, these retirement ages remain unchanged.[14] Moreover, a 2006 survey of almost 20 million retirees by China's Ministry of Human Resources and Social Security found that over half of all workers had retired early, before reaching the statutory minimum retirement age. That study placed the average retirement age at just 54. In short, "China's retirement pattern looks like that of a wealthy European welfare state" (Cui 2016, 45).

In 2016 the minister of human resources and social security revealed that his department was drafting a plan to gradually raise the official retirement ages for men and women to partially counter the drag on economic growth from the shrinking working age cohort of the population.[15] Whether politics will allow raising retirement ages, of course, remains to be seen.

The shrinkage in the working age population over the coming two decades is certain, but its adverse effect on growth can be partially offset through further investment in human capital and a higher retirement age. Thus, this factor is likely to have only a slightly negative effect on growth going forward.

Reversion to the Mean

A final and perhaps the most powerful and pessimistic explanation of China's slowdown is the "reversion to the mean" view articulated by Pritchett and Summers (2014). Their approach is based on mining data on the growth experiences of more than 100 countries for which there are at least 25 years of data. It does not consider specific factors that many economists have used to try to explain cross-country variation in growth rates. Indeed, they argue that both relatively constant features of countries—such as climate, culture, geography, quality of institutions, and openness to the world—and short-term variables—like the outcome of policy reform—are irrelevant in explaining long-term growth. According Pritchett and Summers, any country's current growth has very little power to predict its future growth. In their view "regression to the mean is perhaps the single most robust and empirical relevant fact about cross-national growth rates" and "in developing countries the growth process is marked by sharp discontinuities, with very large accelerations or decelerations of growth being quite common."

---

14. World Bank, Life Expectancy at Birth, Total (Years), https://data.worldbank.org (accessed on August 3, 2016).

15. "Three Issues in Postponing Retirement," *Guangming ribao*, July 26, 2016, www.mohrss.gov.cn/SYrlzyhshbzb/dongtaixinwen/buneiyaowen/201607/t20160726_244221.html (accessed on August 3, 2016).

They identify 28 countries that have experienced episodes of "super rapid" economic growth, defined as a period of eight or more years with per capita growth averaging above 6 percent. The median episode of super rapid economic growth is only nine years. "China's experience from 1977 to 2010 already holds the distinction of being the only instance, quite possibly in the history of mankind, but certainly in the data, with a sustained episode of super rapid (> 6 ppa) growth for more than 32 years" (Pritchett and Summers 2014). By now China's super rapid growth extends 40 years. On their calculation, the two next longest periods of super rapid growth were Taiwan at 6.8 percent for 32 years from 1962 to 1994 and Korea at 7.0 percent for 29 years from 1962 until 1991.

Pritchett and Summers don't explain why China is a substantial outlier in terms of the duration of its super rapid growth. Why will China's growth slow, they ask? Their answer: "Mainly because that is what rapid growth does. Our confidence in the prediction that growth will slow is much larger than our confidence in being able to specify why or how or when exactly it will slow" (Pritchett and Summers 2014).

While Pritchett and Summers do not comment on China's growth slowdown, which was already evident at the time they wrote their paper, their analysis is consistent with the view that the current deceleration in China's growth is long overdue and likely to persist and deepen. They present three main estimates of China's likely per capita growth during the two-decade period 2013–33. For the first estimate they use regression analysis of the data for countries with super rapid growth, considering both their past decades' growth and their initial levels of income in purchasing power parity terms (to allow for convergence) to estimate coefficients that are then used to estimate China's future growth. This methodology, the so-called conditional approach, predicts that China's growth from 2013 through 2033 will be 3.9 percent. The second estimate is based on the observation that the median pace of expansion in countries after an episode of super rapid growth is 2 percent. So the second estimate, which Pritchett and Summers refer to as full convergence, is that China's average growth between 2013 and 2033 will be 2 percent. The third estimate is based on the observation that the average growth deceleration after a period of super rapid growth in other countries was 4.65 percentage points. Applying this deceleration metric to the Chinese case, where the pace of super rapid growth has been about 2 percentage points above the median of other countries that have experienced super rapid growth episodes, Pritchett and Summers opine that China's growth might average 4 percent per capita between 2013 and 2033. They do not offer any judgment as to which of these three estimates is most likely.

Evaluating the reversion to the mean forecast of China's future economic growth is more difficult since this hypothesis is based on a careful analysis of a huge dataset rather than an examination of specific factors that may apply in the Chinese case. Its greatest weakness, in my opinion, is that it does not appear to adequately recognize the extraordinarily low level of per capita economic development in China in 1978, on the eve of its extended period of super rapid economic growth—about 5 percent of the US level measured in terms of purchasing power parity.[16] From this initial low level, 35 years of growth averaging almost 9 percent per capita brought China's level of per capita income measured in purchasing power parity terms to only 25 percent of the US level. After Japan, Taiwan, Korea, and Singapore reached this level of development they continued to grow at rates between 7.7 and 9.3 percent annually over the next 20 years. If China replicates the experience of these countries it still will have another two decades of super rapid growth.

Table 1.1 summarizes the possible contribution of each of the seven factors to China's slowdown since the global financial crisis and, for the four factors that are judged to be persistent, assesses their contribution to China's potential growth. The first three explanations are transitory and thus not likely to weigh negatively on China's potential growth.

The fourth and fifth explanations of China's slowing growth—the slowing pace of economic reform and the rising burden of China's debt—are closely tied to domestic economic policy. If current policy emphasizing the role of the state and state-owned companies and diminishing the role of the market continues and no reforms improve productivity among state firms, growth is likely to slow further. Because state firms claim a disproportionately large share of bank credit and use the resources very inefficiently, these explanations are closely tied to the Michael Pettis argument that the rising burden of debt will further slow China's growth.

As already argued, it is easy to overstate the influence of demographic factors, but the shrinking labor force certainly is a slightly negative factor weighing on China's potential growth. Reversion to the mean, the seventh factor, is clearly a large negative in assessing China's potential growth.

---

16. Given China's very low initial level of development, one would expect the conditional estimate of China's future growth, based on regression analysis that includes the initial level of development and thus allows for the effect of convergence, to be higher than the unconditional estimate. Instead the two estimates are quite close, indeed the conditional estimate, 3.9 percent, is slightly below the unconditional estimate of 4.0 percent.

Figure 1.2   Private consumption as a share of GDP, 1978–2016

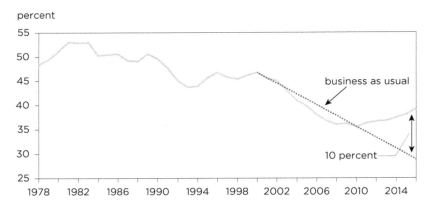

percent

Sources: National Bureau of Statistics of China (2017e, 73–74); National Bureau of Statistics of China, data.stats.gov.cn (accessed on September 5, 2017); National Bureau of Statistics of China via Wind Financial Information (accessed on August 1, 2018).

The Rebalancing Strategy

The Pettis view that China is unlikely to rebalance its sources of growth and that continued reliance on debt-fueled expansion will soon drag down the pace of expansion to the low single digits requires a more extensive evaluation. The pessimists notwithstanding, the evidence shows that economic rebalancing has been under way since around 2010, and without this progress on rebalancing, growth would have slowed even more.

The progress can be judged from three perspectives. The first is the expenditure perspective, i.e., the relative importance of private consumption expenditure, government consumption expenditure, investment expenditure, and net exports in driving economic growth. The second is the production perspective, i.e., the relative contributions of the primary sector (agriculture, forestry, animal husbandry, and fisheries), secondary sector (mining, manufacturing, utilities, and construction), and tertiary sector (services) to GDP. The third perspective looks at the relative shares of national income accruing to labor and capital. As outlined below, on each of these perspectives rebalancing has made measurable, sustained progress starting in about 2010.

As shown in figure 1.2, the share of private consumption expenditure in China's GDP in 2000 was only 2 percentage points lower than at the beginning of the reform era in 1978. After 2000 the share steadily declined for 10 years. By 2010 the share had fallen to an all-time low of only 36 percent, 11 percentage points lower than in 2000. But since 2010 growth of private consumption has consistently outpaced growth of GDP, so its share had risen

Figure 1.3 Services share of GDP, 1978–2016

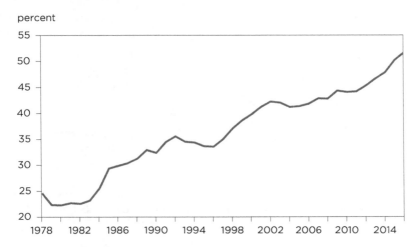

percent

Sources: National Bureau of Statistics of China (2017e, 58); National Bureau of Statistics of China, data.stats.gov.cn (accessed on September 5, 2017); National Bureau of Statistics of China via Wind Financial Information (accessed on August 1, 2018).

to 39 percent by 2016. While in absolute terms this is only a small increase, compared with the trend of the previous decade, labeled "business as usual" in the figure, private consumption expenditure has strengthened substantially.

Government consumption also reached a peak in 2000 and then, like private consumption, weakened for the next decade. It too has strengthened since 2010, albeit by a smaller amount. On the other hand, the share of investment expenditure, which peaked in 2010 at 48 percent of GDP, had fallen to 44 percent by 2016 (National Bureau of Statistics of China 2017e, 73).[17] Net exports peaked at 8.7 percent of GDP in 2007 but since have fallen steadily, reaching a low of 2.2 percent in 2016. In short, all four components of expenditure have been moving in the right direction since 2010.

The production perspective also shows evidence that rebalancing is proceeding apace. One piece of evidence is in the recently expanding role of the service sector. As shown in figure 1.3, the share of services in China's GDP almost doubled in the first two decades or so of reform, reaching a peak of 42 percent in 2002. This period of rapid services growth reflected recovery from the era of economic planning prior to 1978, which assigned a low priority to services. But after 2002, government policies hindered the growth of services so that its share of GDP rose only 2 percentage points between 2002 and

---

17. Investment here is measured by gross domestic capital formation, not fixed asset investment.

Figure 1.4 GDP growth and services growth, 1978-2016

percent (measured in constant prices)

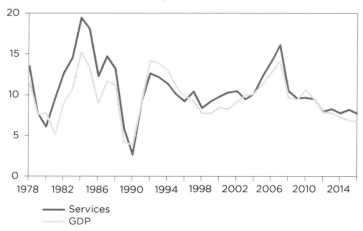

Services
GDP

Source: National Bureau of Statistics of China via Wind Financial Information (accessed on August 1, 2018).

2010 (Lardy 2012, 54). Since then, services growth has revived and by 2016 its share had increased to 52 percent of GDP (National Bureau of Statistics of China 2017b). Part of this more robust recent performance is due to relative price trends; services inflation ran ahead of other indicators of inflation after 2010. But measured in real terms (i.e., constant prices), as shown in figure 1.4, on an annual basis, services growth has slightly but persistently outpaced the growth of GDP beginning in 2013.[18] Concomitantly, the share of industry in GDP has fallen since its peak of 42 percent in 2006, though some of this decline reflects deflation of industrial prices in 2012–16. Measuring both in real terms, the growth of industry began to persistently lag the growth of services starting in 2013 (National Bureau of Statistics of China 2017e, 62).

Data from the income perspective support the same conclusion—rebalancing has been underway for some time. During the decade of imbalanced growth labor compensation as a share of GDP fell from 54 percent in 2002 to 47 percent in 2011, when it bottomed out (National Bureau of Statistics of China 2012, 82–83; 2013, 80–81). By 2015 the share had recovered to 52 percent of GDP (National Bureau of Statistics of China 2017e, 81–82). This trend is quite unusual when compared with trends in industrialized econo-

---

18. This assessment is disputed by Naughton (2016b, 59–60), who believes that the National Bureau of Statistics of China uses flawed price indices that result in an overstatement of the growth of services in real terms.

Figure 1.5 Household disposable income as a share of GDP, 1992–2015

percent

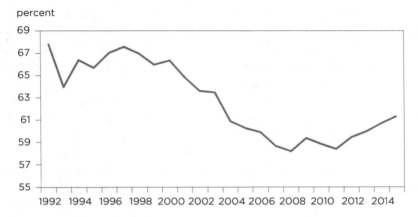

Sources: National Bureau of Statistics of China (2017e, 82); National Bureau of Statistics of China, data.stats.gov.cn (accessed on September 5, 2017); National Bureau of Statistics of China via Wind Financial Information (accessed on August 1, 2018).

mies, where labor compensation as a share of GDP has been flat in recent years.[19]

As shown in figure 1.5, household disposable income as a share of GDP also has risen from a low of 58 percent in 2008 to 61 percent in 2015 (National Bureau of Statistics of China 2012, 88–89; 2017e, 81–82).[20]

Thus, all three approaches—expenditure, production, and income—show that rebalancing has been underway since 2010 or 2011 for all the metrics examined.

Explaining the Rebalancing Progress

Several factors have contributed to the rebalancing process summarized above. They can be divided into those driving the transition from the demand side and those from the supply side.

---

19. The weighted average labor compensation as a share of GDP in OECD countries was unchanged between 2011 and 2015. OECD data are available at www.oecd.org (accessed on December 14, 2017).

20. Disposable income has risen less than wage income because the growth of income of household businesses has lagged the growth of wage income.

Demand Side Factors

These factors include demographics, rapid economic growth that has propelled China into the ranks of upper-middle-income countries as defined by the World Bank, strengthening of the social safety net, reduced financial repression, and the relatively labor-intensive nature of services production. Each of these factors, which contribute to increased consumption demand, stronger service sector growth, and rising labor compensation as a share of GDP, is either structural, and thus will endure, or the result of government policy that is likely to persist. Thus, the conclusion is that demand side factors will continue to work to reinforce the rebalancing that is already underway.

Demographics is almost certain to reinforce the trend of rising wages, which has been evident in China for many years, as well as to push down the household saving rate. China's working age population peaked in 2013, largely because of the one-child policy adopted in 1980. Although the government slightly adjusted this policy over the years and then eased it significantly in 2015, China's working age population will continue to decline for at least two decades and perhaps longer, depending on how much fertility responds to the 2015 policy change. Other things being equal, slower growth of the working age population will translate into a more rapid growth of real wages.

The World Bank reclassified China from the lower-middle-income to the upper-middle-income category in 2011. As countries approach this status and incomes continue to rise, households invariably begin to shift their consumption patterns in relative terms away from food, clothing, and many other goods and more toward services, a regularity first observed by statistician Charles Engel in the 19th century and thus known as Engel's law. This pattern is already evident in China, reflected in the relatively faster growth of household consumption expenditure on health care, education, entertainment, travel, and other services, while the share of expenditure on food, clothing, and most other goods is declining. The share of expenditure on services overall rose from 44 percent in 2002 to 49 percent by 2012 (National Bureau of Statistics of China 2006, 80; 2015, 88).[21] But this share is still far less than in high-income countries like the United States, where services account for two-thirds of household consumption expenditures.[22] As wages and incomes

---

21. The services share of household consumption is calculated using data from China's input-output table, which is updated every two or three years and then published with a lag of several additional years.

22. US Department of Commerce, Bureau of Economic Analysis, www.bea.gov (accessed on June 23, 2017).

Figure 1.6 Household saving as a share of disposable income, 1992-2015

percent

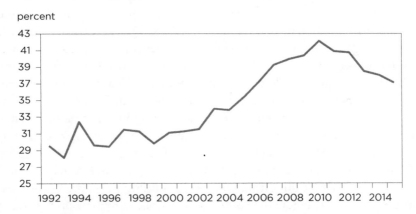

Sources: National Bureau of Statistics of China (2017e, 82); National Bureau of Statistics of China, data.stats.gov.cn (accessed on September 5, 2017); National Bureau of Statistics of China via Wind Financial Information (accessed on August 1, 2018).

in China continue to rise, the share of expenditure on services will gradually approach the level in high-income countries.

The strengthening of the social safety net will also increase household consumption because it will likely encourage the Chinese, who are prodigious savers, to save less. As shown in figure 1.6, household saving as a share of after-tax household income peaked at 42 percent in 2010 but since has gradually declined, reaching 37 percent by 2015.[23] Part of this decline is undoubtedly the result of a strengthened social safety net, which includes a rural cooperative medical insurance system, initiated on a trial basis in a few regions in 2003; an urban basic medical insurance scheme to cover urban residents without formal employment, launched in 2007;[24] a rural pension scheme, again initiated on a trial basis in a few locations starting in 2008; and a pension scheme for

---

23. Data on household saving come from the flow of funds, which is compiled by the National Bureau of Statistics of China but published with a considerable lag. The data for 2015 are in the *2017 Statistical Yearbook*, published in November 2017.

24. Medical insurance programs for employees of state enterprises and the government were established in the early 1950s. The scheme for enterprise employees was expanded to encompass firms other than state-owned. The two schemes were merged in the early 1990s to form the urban employee basic medical insurance scheme.

nonworking urban residents, launched a few years later.[25] The rural pension scheme was operating in one-fourth of all counties by 2010. The number of participants in the two pension schemes, which were merged in 2012, rose from about 100 million in 2010 to just over 500 million participants in 2015.

The longest-standing component of the strengthened social safety net, the rural cooperative medical insurance scheme, is worth examining in some detail. It began quite modestly, requiring individual contributions of only RMB10 annually, which the government matched with RMB40 per participant. These funds were pooled at the county level and used to partially reimburse rural residents for costs of significant medical expenses, typically associated with treatments requiring hospitalization. The program was voluntary for individuals but takeup was quite rapid as rural residents observed relatives and neighbors receiving significant reimbursement for hospital costs. Within five years the program had more than 800 million enrollees, more than 90 percent of the eligible population. By 2014 the enrollment rate reached 99 percent of the eligible population (National Bureau of Statistics of China 2015, 743).

Initially the program was able to reimburse only a modest share of hospital costs, an estimated 30 percent in 2007 (World Bank 2008, 89), which rose to 40 to 50 percent in most areas by around 2010 (World Bank 2012, 333). Higher reimbursement rates and, over time, increased coverage to include outpatient services were made possible by rising enrollment rates, increased individual premium payments, and much larger government financial contributions. By 2011 the government contributed RMB200 per participant, which rose further in annual increments to reach RMB450 per person in 2017 (Ministry of Finance 2011, State Council Information Office 2017). The government's white paper on public health anticipated the average inpatient and outpatient reimbursement rates to rise to 70 and 50 percent, respectively, in 2017 (State Council Information Office 2017).

As noted briefly above, demographics will also contribute to a declining household saving rate. A decline in fertility, starting in the 1960s and deepening after the one-child policy was adopted, led to an increase in the working age population relative to the total population. This trend is captured in the so-called dependency ratio, the ratio of the elderly and young population to the working age population, which fell from 0.8 as reform was getting underway in the early 1980s to a low of about 0.35 in 2010. This so-called demographic dividend is widely believed to have contributed to an increase

---

25. The latter scheme covered urban residents who were never employed in an urban work unit or were employed for such a short period that they were not eligible for the urban employee basic pension insurance program.

in the household saving rate.[26] The reason is simple: With fewer dependents a working age person typically saves a larger share of income. But as a population ages, a growing share starts drawing down their accumulated savings, thus reducing the household saving rate. China's dependency ratio has been rising since 2010 and, based on United Nations fertility projections, will continue to rise through at least 2050, further reducing the household saving rate (Golley, Tyers, and Zhou 2016). The International Monetary Fund (IMF 2017a, 14) estimates that the aging of the population will reduce the household saving rate by 6 percentage points between 2015 and 2030.

The medical and pension programs noted above have almost certainly contributed to the decline in the household saving rate observed since 2010. The government has been enhancing these programs for more than a decade and will continue to do so. Because of these programs, plus the aging of the population, the household saving rate will continue to decline for many years and the share of household income devoted to consumption will gradually rise further.

The fourth demand side factor that is favorable for the continued rebalancing of China's economic growth is an easing of financial repression. One important indicator of financial repression is low or negative real deposit rates paid on household savings. In China households faced substantial repression starting in 2004 as real bank deposit rates plunged. In 2004–13 the average real deposit rate was more than 300 basis points below the average deposit rate in 1997–2003 (Lardy 2014, 129–30). Financial repression reduced consumption through two channels. First, lower interest rates on deposits reduced household income below the levels it would have attained in a more liberal financial environment. For example, if real interest rates on household bank deposits in the first half of 2008 had been the same as in 2002, households would have earned RMB690 billion more in interest on their RMB18,680 billion in bank savings deposits. That was the equivalent of 5.3 percent of GDP in the first half of 2008 (Goldstein and Lardy 2009, 38).

In addition, evidence shows that the decline in the return to savings associated with financial repression in the second half of the 2000s led Chinese households to save more to have sufficient funds for retirement, to finance a child's education, or for medical emergencies (Chamon and Prasad 2008, 19; IMF 2011, 34; Nabar 2011). In China, the primary form of household savings

---

26. A contrary view is expressed in Chamon and Prasad (2008), who argue that demographic factors played only a limited role in the sharp rise in the household saving rate between 1990 and 2005. They point to sharply increased housing-related savings and increased precautionary savings because of uncertainty associated with the restructuring of state-owned enterprises.

is bank deposits. Households offset a decline in the return on these savings by saving more in order to reach their cumulative saving target as close as possible to the initially planned date. In short, financial repression both reduced household income and increased household savings from that lower income, creating a double-barreled negative effect on household consumption.

But in the last few years, financial repression from the perspective of households has moderated. Real bank deposit rates have consistently been positive since the first quarter of 2012.[27] Yu'ebao, a money market fund launched by Alibaba in mid-2013 and now the world's largest such fund, offers households higher interest rates than banks; banks, trust companies, and other nonbank financial institutions offer so-called wealth management products not subject to interest rate limitations; and in October 2015 the central bank eliminated the cap on bank deposit rates that had been in place for decades.

Banks also faced financial repression in the 2000s, as reflected in the sharp rise in the share of their deposits that they were required to hold at the central bank at a very low interest rate. This was a function of China's exchange rate policy at the time. As noted earlier in this chapter, the central bank was charged with intervening in the foreign exchange market, buying up huge quantities of foreign exchange to prevent the renminbi from appreciating. As a result of this intervention China's foreign exchange reserves, which were a modest US$400 billion at the end of 2003, reached an annual year-end peak of $3,843 billion in 2014 (China Banking Society 2013, 352; 2016, 399). The purchases of foreign exchange considerably increased the domestic money supply. To avoid inflation, the central bank largely offset this increase in money supply by requiring the banks to hand over a growing and ultimately unusually large share of the deposits that they took in. The central bank repeatedly raised the required reserve ratio that it imposes on commercial banks, from 7 percent in late 2003 to a peak of 21.5 percent starting in June 2011.[28] Starting in 2003 the central bank also sold its own renminbi-denominated central bank bills into the domestic money market as part of its sterilization

---

27. The average real deposit rate from the beginning of 2012, when real rates went above zero, to October 2015, when the cap on deposit rates was lifted by the central bank, was 1.1 percent, compared with −0.5 percent from 2004 through 2011. As previously noted, this assessment is based on the one-year benchmark bank deposit rate, with allowance when relevant for the flexibility banks had to pay a premium over the benchmark rate.

28. Wind Financial Information. The required reserve ratio was uniform across all financial institutions until September 2008, when the central bank instituted a lower rate for small and medium depository institutions. Initially the preferential rate was 1 percentage point less, but since December 2008 the preferential rate has been 2 percentage points less. The rates given in the text are for large depository institutions.

campaign. The stock of these outstanding bonds, which were allocated on a quota system to individual Chinese banks, reached a peak of RMB4.6 trillion at the end of 2008 (National Bureau of Statistics of China 2010a, 738).

Again, the current state of all these indicators suggests that financial repression has eased. The central bank is no longer buying up foreign exchange; indeed in 2015 it began to sell foreign exchange, leading to a drop in foreign exchange reserves to US$3,011 billion by the end of 2016 (National Bureau of Statistics of China 2017e, 595). Selling foreign exchange reduces the domestic money supply, which the central bank has offset through two mechanisms. First, by the first quarter of 2016 it had lowered the required reserve ratio eight times, bringing the rate for major banks to 17 percent.[29] Second, after 2008 the magnitude of new central bank bill issuance was less than the magnitude of maturing bonds, allowing the stock outstanding to run off to only RMB776 billion by the end of 2013 (National Bureau of Statistics of China 2015, 638). This process accelerated after 2013 when the central bank stopped issuing new bonds, extinguishing the entire stock of these bonds in June 2017 (People's Bank of China 2017).

The last of the demand side factors that have contributed to economic rebalancing is the relative labor intensity of services production. China's National Bureau of Statistics calculates that an RMB1 million increase in real value added in services creates 9.1 new jobs, while the same increase in value added in industry and construction creates only 7.5 new jobs (Guo 2017a). Thus, as the service sector expands faster than industry and construction, more jobs are created, further increasing household income and expenditure on services, which generates more jobs in services, and the cycle continues.

Three of the five demand side factors just analyzed—demographics, increasing share of services in household consumption expenditure, and labor intensity of services—are structural, meaning they are not subject to policy reversal and thus will persist. The two other demand side factors—expansion of the social safety net and reduced financial repression—reflect changes in Chinese government policy. The buildout of the social safety net started more than a decade ago and has progressed steadily since. Given the high level of voluntary participation in the various insurance and pension programs, the government will likely continue strengthening the social safety net. Even though China's leaders do not stand in popular elections, they are likely to continue policies that generate goodwill and popular support.

The easing of financial repression ultimately reflects China's abandonment of a mercantilist trade policy pursued via an undervalued currency. In 2015

---

29. Data are from Wind Financial Information.

the IMF came to the judgment that "substantial real effective appreciation has brought the renminbi to a level that is no longer undervalued" (IMF 2015, 1). The following year the Fund opined that "the renminbi remains broadly in line with fundamentals" (IMF 2016a). William Cline reached a similar conclusion somewhat earlier. His earliest estimate was that in mid-2008 the renminbi was undervalued in real effective terms by almost 20 percent (Cline and Williamson 2008). By April 2014 he estimated that the degree of undervaluation had fallen to only 1 percent (Cline 2014). China may return to a policy of significant undervaluation of the renminbi but it seems unlikely now that Chinese households are benefiting from higher real interest rates on bank deposits and have access to a range of new financial assets that generate even higher real returns.

Supply Side Factors

In addition to the five demand side factors analyzed above, trends on the supply side are driving more balanced economic growth. These include an exchange rate that is no longer undervalued, tax reforms that are reducing longstanding discrimination against the tertiary sector, and the gradual opening of parts of the tertiary sector that had long been closed to private investment.

One aspect of the exchange rate factor has already been discussed above. Financial repression associated with an undervalued currency had a double-barreled negative effect on consumption—lower total household income and a higher saving rate from this reduced income. Supply-side effects of currency undervaluation are also important. An undervalued currency for most of the 2000s made exports more profitable than domestic sales—foreign currencies earned by selling goods abroad could be converted into renminbi at a more favorable rate. And since undervaluation made imports more expensive in domestic currency, domestic producers of goods competing with these imports were able to charge higher prices on their domestic sales. As a result, domestic goods that competed with imports were also more profitable. Because almost all of China's exports and most of its imports are manufactured goods, an undervalued renminbi boosted the profitability of manufactures at the expense of services. An undervalued currency, in effect, was an implicit tax on the production of services. This was an important reason why industry growth was so high and service sector production was stagnating in the early 2000s, when the renminbi first became undervalued.

The appreciation of the renminbi, starting slowly in July 2005 and more rapidly beginning in 2010, has largely eliminated the implicit tax on services.

By October 2017 the currency had appreciated 45 percent on a real, trade-weighted basis.[30]

The tax piece of the story is very straightforward. In the 1980s China gradually replaced its product tax with a value-added tax (VAT) on manufactured goods and imports and introduced a business tax on services. China's business tax is levied on top-line income, whereas a VAT is levied only on the difference between a firm's sales and its cost of nonfactor inputs. For firms with a narrow profit margin, the effective burden of a 5 or 6 percent business tax can be huge. Even loss-making firms were required to pay the business tax on their sales revenue, increasing their pre–income tax losses.

The government rolled out the VAT for services in January 2012. The pilot, which was initially limited to Shanghai and covered only a few services, was gradually expanded both in scope and geography. By August 2013 the government had implemented the VAT on some services nationwide and by May 2016 expanded the sectoral coverage to encompass all services. At the same time the government abolished the business tax on services throughout China, finally putting services production on a more equal footing with manufacturing. This reform reduced the tax burden on services firms by about RMB500 billion, an amount equal to 1.5 percent of value added in services in 2015 (State Administration of Taxation 2016).[31]

Finally, on the supply side, the gradual opening of parts of the service sector to private firms is contributing to the sector's expansion. As shown in the next chapter, private service firms in general are far more efficient, as measured by return on assets, than state firms. Thus, as the share of private investment in services rises, growth of the sector accelerates. Private firms were able to move into services such as retail and restaurants relatively early in the reform process. But the share of private investment in modern business services, long relatively closed to private firms, expanded significantly between 2012 and 2015 (figure 1.7). Nonetheless, the opening of the service sector to private firms is limited—investment in modern business services accounts for well under 10 percent of total investment in services.

---

30. The Bank for International Settlements (BIS) real effective exchange rate index rose from 83.5 in June 2007 to 121.4 in October 2017, a cumulative appreciation of 45 percent. See www.bis.org/statistics/eer.htm (accessed on March 23, 2018).

31. The reported savings accumulated during the eight months from May, when the business tax on services was eliminated. If we assume that the value added in services was the same in every month of the year, the RMB500 billion in savings would represent 2.6 percent of value added during the eight-month period.

Figure 1.7 Share of private investment in modern business services, 2012–16

percent

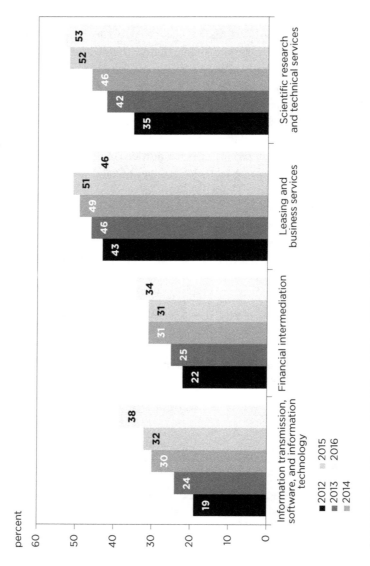

Information transmission, software, and information technology: 2012: 19, 2013: 24, 2014: 30, 2015: 32, 2016: 38

Financial intermediation: 2012: 22, 2013: 25, 2014: 31, 2015: 31, 2016: 34

Leasing and business services: 2012: 43, 2013: 46, 2014: 49, 2015: 51, 2016: 46

Scientific research and technical services: 2012: 35, 2013: 42, 2014: 46, 2015: 52, 2016: 53

■ 2012   ■ 2013   ■ 2014   ■ 2015   ■ 2016

Sources: National Bureau of Statistics of China (2017e, 313); National Bureau of Statistics of China, data.stats.gov.cn (accessed on September 5, 2017); National Bureau of Statistics of China via Wind Financial Information (accessed on August 1, 2018).

China's slowing output growth and declining total factor productivity since the global financial crisis are not the inevitable slowing of a more mature, upper-middle-income country. As measured by exchange rates, in 2017 China ranked only 76th globally in terms of per capita income and, as measured by purchasing power parity, China's per capita income is only about a quarter of the level of the United States.[32] "There remains considerable room for China to continue catching up" (IMF 2018, 4). Rather, the single largest explanation of China's slowing growth is that before the global financial crisis growth was above potential because of an unprecedented surge in its trade surplus. The decline in that surplus to a much smaller, more sustainable level slowed China's growth, but this drag on growth has now waned.

The other most important factor, detailed in the next chapter, is the slowing pace of economic reform and the steadily deteriorating performance of state-owned enterprises since the global financial crisis. The resurgence of the role of the state in resource allocation, reflected in the creation of the State-Owned Assets Supervision and Administration Commission of the State Council (SASAC); the proliferation of industrial policies favoring state over private and foreign firms; and the increasing access of state firms to bank loans ironically have coincided with a marked weakening in the performance of state companies. The return on assets of state firms in industry and services fell by two-thirds and two-fifths, respectively, between 2007 and 2016. In addition, the combination of weak private property rights and the increasing propensity of banks to lend to state companies has discouraged entrepreneurs from investing, which reduced the pace of private relative to state investment after 2011 led to the first ever decline in the share of private investment beginning in 2016. Progress in rebalancing the sources of China's growth, with services and private consumption assuming increasing roles as the growth of investment and exports moderates, has partially offset the drag on growth from the negative factors just summarized.

---

32. As measured by purchasing power parity, China ranked 82nd (World GDP Per Capita Ranking 2017, https://knoema.com/sijweyg/world-gdp-per-capita-ranking-2017-data-and-charts-forecast [accessed on March 15, 2018]).

2

China's Convergence Potential

The deteriorating financial performance of China's state firms and their increasing claim on resources have slowed China's growth in recent years to below its potential rate. Looking long term, however, assuming a reasonably favorable global environment, China has a substantial opportunity to converge closer to per capita income levels of developed countries.

This chapter focuses on the potential for convergence across firms with different types of ownership. State firms in China are generally far less efficient than private firms and control a large and rapidly growing quantity of assets, which if used more efficiently would greatly improve China's economic performance. Measured by return on assets, the efficiency of state firms has declined massively compared with what it was in 2007, while the returns of private firms are higher than they were just before the global financial crisis. As a result, the gap between returns of private and state firms is at an all-time high. If the efficiency of state firms approached that of private firms or if state assets that remain underperforming could be acquired by more productive private firms, China's growth over the medium term would receive a major boost, borrowing by state firms would moderate, and risks in the financial system stemming from unusually large credit flows to state companies would be measurably reduced.

Approaches to Analyzing China's Growth Potential

The *production function approach* is the most common framework for explaining a country's past economic growth and estimating the pace of its future expansion. It typically relies on a Cobb-Douglas production function, in which growth is a function of the pace of expansion of the capital stock and the labor force as well as improvements in human capital and the growth of total factor productivity, with the latter estimated as the residual of growth unexplained by the aforementioned factors. After decomposing the historical sources of growth of GDP, a forward-looking estimate of the same is constructed by first estimating the pace of expansion of the four individual growth determinants and then using these estimates to generate projections of GDP growth.

This supply side approach is extremely data intensive and invariably requires innumerable judgments and assumptions. To start with, it requires reasonably accurate historical data on output, the stock of capital, and the size of the labor force, as well as data that attempt to capture improvements in human capital, such as years of schooling of the labor force. Even if one constructs reasonably accurate measures of these variables, forward projection requires many judgments. The size of the potential workforce over a decade or two is easily estimated. But anticipating how the labor force participation rate will evolve is more difficult. Anticipating the growth of the country's capital stock or improvements in human capital is even more difficult. Finally, any estimate of future growth of total factor productivity is fraught with even greater challenges.

Several studies have used this approach to deconstruct China's growth over various periods and to offer growth forecasts. The study by Dwight Perkins and Tom Rawski (2008) is one of the most comprehensive and thoughtful. Although compiling data on the capital stock and estimating improvements in human capital were far from easy, their major challenge in forecasting China's growth was assessing future productivity growth, which they estimated accounted for fully two-fifths of China's economic expansion from the beginning of economic reform in 1978 until 2005. They concluded that China would be unlikely to sustain the 3.8 percent annual productivity growth attained in 1978–2005, and even achieving the 3.1 to 3.2 percent annual productivity growth recorded in 1995–2005 would be a challenge. They estimated that China's GDP growth would be between 6 and 8 percent in 2006–15 and between 5 and 7 percent in 2016–25.

A second approach to analyzing growth potential over the medium term relies on the *hypothesis of convergence*, which is much more parsimonious than the production function approach. The convergence hypothesis argues that poor countries can grow faster than rich countries, creating a pattern of catch-up. A country that is far from the technological frontier, usually measured by the gap between the country's per capita income and that of the most developed economies, can borrow and adapt advanced technologies, best practices, and knowledge from more developed countries (McKinsey Global Institute

2015). This absorption and adaption involves some combination of inward foreign direct investment and joint ventures with foreign firms with advanced technologies, purchases of foreign equipment, technology licensing arrangements, and other forms of technology acquisition. Modern standards of financial disclosure, transparency, and corporate governance can also be borrowed. There is thus no need to develop these advanced technologies and governance standards from scratch. The basic concept of convergence, sometimes referred to as the "latecomer's advantage," was initially developed decades ago by Alexander Gerschenkron (1951, reprinted in 1966).

While the hypothesis of convergence is simpler and perhaps intuitively appealing as an explanation of growth over long periods, very few countries have been able to meaningfully close the gap in per capita income with developed economies. This reminds us that convergence is about potential growth, not a forecast of actual growth. Indeed, from the 1950s until about 2000 the gap between the levels of per capita income in emerging-market and developing economies and in developed economies did not shrink but rather expanded steadily (Rodrik 2011). Disaggregating by region, growth in most countries in Latin America and Africa was particularly slow compared with that in developed economies, so gaps there widened the most. Only in Asia, starting in the late 1970s, did the gap close steadily, largely because China's growth accelerated after 1978.

After 2000, consistent with the convergence hypothesis, developing economies as a group grew faster than developed economies so that by 2008 their growth averaged 4 percentage points above that of developed economies (Rodrik 2011). The convergence hypothesis seemed to be confirmed. Because of this convergence, global growth accelerated compared with earlier decades, and some commentators argued that the pattern of global growth had changed permanently and the gap between developed and developing economies would steadily shrink.

This optimism was not entirely warranted. In its 2016 *Global Economic Prospects* report, the World Bank (2016) showed that the pace of economic convergence slowed dramatically in the wake of the global financial crisis. The share of the 114 economies classified by the Bank as emerging-market and developing economies that were catching up with the US level of per capita GDP shot up from just under 30 percent in 1999 to 90 percent at the peak of 2008. But by 2015 the share of these countries catching up with the United States had fallen to under 50 percent. Based on growth trends in 2003–08, the most promising 21 economies in the larger group, so-called emerging markets, on average would have caught up with the US level of per capita GDP in 2015 in 42.3 years. Based on their relative performance in 2013–15, the Bank estimated that it would take these economies 67.7 years to catch up with the United States.[1]

But the more rapid pace of convergence observed in 2000–08 may yet reemerge. In its 2018 *Global Economic Prospects* report, the World Bank estimates that the potential growth of emerging-market and developing economies in the 2018–27 decade will be 3 percentage points higher than potential growth of developed economies (World Bank 2018a, 160). If this potential is realized, it would shorten the time for convergence to the US level of per capita GDP in 2017.

The potential for international convergence is greater when a country exhibits especially large internal, domestic disparities. For example, domestic firms with lower productivity in a particular industry could converge toward the frontier represented by the most efficient domestic firms in the same industry, pushing up the country's economic growth. Another dimension of domestic convergence is regional. China is marked by large productivity gaps across regions and within industries. Reducing these gaps would also be positive for sustaining China's economic growth.

International Convergence in Asia

Figure 2.1 shows that Japan in 1951, Singapore in 1967, Taiwan in 1975, and South Korea in 1977 were all at the same level of economic development relative to the United States, about one-quarter, as measured by per capita GDP in purchasing power parity terms. Each of these economies then expanded rapidly for 20 years at average annual rates between 7.7 and 9.3 percent. At the end of the two-decade period, this growth, which was much more rapid than that in the United States, allowed South Korea, Taiwan, and Singapore to converge to about half the per capita GDP level of the United States (again measured at purchasing power parity terms) and Japan to converge to about two-thirds of the US level. Each of these Asian economies thus avoided what is sometimes referred to as the middle-income trap and after 20 years of rapid growth they transitioned to become high-income economies.

China's per capita GDP in 2014, again in purchasing power parity terms, was one-fourth that of the United States in the same year, the same as the starting point of each of the four economies shown in figure 2.1. The world already contains the technology that potentially can yield a per capita income four times China's current level (Davies and Raskovic 2018, 87). "Visitors on the *maglev* [line from one of the city's airports] to Shanghai may not see this,

---

1. Shawn Donnan, "Catch-Up of Emerging Nations Set Back 'Decades,'" *Financial Times*, June 8, 2016, 5.

Figure 2.1 China's catch-up potential from a historic perspective

percent   percent

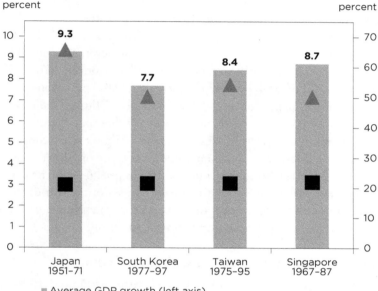

■ Average GDP growth (left axis)
▲ Per capita GDP relative to US, end of period (right axis)
■ Per capita GDP relative to US, beginning of period (right axis)

Source: Angus Maddison Database, www.ggdc.net/Maddison/historical_
statistics/horizontalfile_02-2010.xls (accessed on August 1, 2018).

but those on the overnight bus to rural Anhui realise there's still a long way to go" (Hubbard 2014). If China replicates the experience of the four economies in figure 2.1, it will have another couple of decades of growth that would be judged quite rapid in comparative terms (Lin 2013). This analysis points out that although China has already grown rapidly for a record-breaking number of years, this growth began at an extremely low level of per capita income relative to the frontier—only about 5 percent of the then prevailing level in the United States.[2]

Japan's convergence toward US per capita income starting in 1951 was unusual in two dimensions, perhaps undermining the relevance of its successful convergence for China. First, the devastation of World War II left Japan's per capita income in 1945 at just under half its 1940 peak. Second, its economic catch-up was facilitated by an initial high level of human capital relative to its per capita income (Noland and Pack 2003, 24–25). Japan's per capita

---

2. According to the Penn World Tables.

GDP in 1951, when it reached one-quarter of the US level, was still below the 1940 peak, a level that was not reattained until the mid-1950s.[3] In short, the first five years of Japan's 20-year growth in 1951–71 were pure recovery. In contrast, in 1978, when China's rapid growth began, its per capita GDP was already the highest on record, roughly two times its peak level of 1938.

The cases of Korea, Taiwan, and Singapore, however, are quite different. Korea and Taiwan, like Japan, suffered massive losses during World War II; their per capita GDP levels in 1945 were less than half the previous peak. The levels reached one-quarter of the US level only about three decades after the end of the war, in 1977 and 1975, respectively. At that time their levels of per capita GDP were about two and a half times pre-war peak levels. Singapore, as a tiny city state, is less relevant for an economy the size of China's, but when its per capita GDP reached one-quarter of the US level in 1967 its per capita GDP was almost half again as large as in 1950. In short, the two-decade-long impressive growth performances of these three economies shown in figure 2.1 can't be attributed to recovery from wartime devastation.

Disparities within Groups of Chinese Firms

The differences in the performance of Chinese firms within industries, across regions, and across ownership arrangements in China are unusually large and have widened considerably in recent years. Wide heterogeneity in firm performance within industries but across ownership types indicates resource misallocation. Thus, appropriate reforms might lead underperforming firms to converge toward productivity levels of firms at the frontier, increasing productivity and output even if firms at the domestic frontier were not converging toward international levels of productivity.

For example, Hsieh and Klenow (2009) examined Chinese plant-level data and found substantial dispersion in the marginal products of both capital and labor among firms in 86 distinct manufacturing subsectors, suggesting the potential for gains if capital and labor were reallocated to reduce this dispersion. Rather than estimating the productivity and output gains that could be achieved if marginal products across firms were fully equalized within each of the 86 subsectors, they estimated the potential gains based on equalization of marginal products to the same extent observed within the same subsectors in the United States, implicitly recognizing that gaps remain in marginal prod-

---

3. Information on the levels of per capita GDP in this and the following paragraphs is from *Historical Statistics for the World Economy: 1-2003*, www.ggdc.net/maddison/historical_statistics/horizontal-file_03-2007.xls.

ucts across firms within individual manufacturing sectors even in a comparatively undistorted, predominantly market-based economy. They found that reducing marginal product differentials among firms within individual industries to the levels observed in the United States would have increased total factor productivity in Chinese manufacturing by 30 percent in 2005. That would have generated a two-thirds increase in manufacturing output. Since manufacturing in 2005 accounted for a third of China's GDP, the postulated output gain would have boosted China's GDP by more than a fifth.

Similar firm-level data for Chinese mining, utilities, construction, and service firms are not available, but given that these companies operate in the same economic environment as manufacturing firms, the dispersion in the marginal products of capital and labor among firms within the same line of business probably is also large. Since these other components accounted for over half of GDP in 2005, if these hypothesized marginal product differentials within these components had also been reduced, the gain in China's GDP in 2005 would have been much more than one-fifth (National Bureau of Statistics of China 2007, 65).

Using a similar approach, the IMF (2017b, 26) estimated that if the productivity distribution of Chinese firms converged to that of countries with a more efficient productivity distribution, it would generate productivity gains that would raise China's long-term growth potential by between 0.7 and 1.2 percentage points per year.

State versus Private Firms

Several studies analyze the efficiency of resource use across firms of different ownership types. One of the earliest is by David Dollar and Shang-Jin Wei (2007). Based on data for 2002–04 collected in a survey of 12,400 firms in 200 cities, they calculated the dispersion in returns to capital across firm ownership types and found that state ownership is systematically associated with lower returns to capital.[4] They estimated that the efficiency gains from eliminating the dispersion in marginal returns to capital between state and private firms would raise China's GDP by 5 percent. They suggested that with a more efficient allocation of capital China could achieve the same rate of growth as it would achieve if the share of output devoted to investment were reduced by 5

---

4. Dollar and Wei appropriately classified firms based on ownership shares rather than by firm registration status.

percentage points of GDP, allowing for a meaningful increase in consumption and living standards for Chinese households.[5]

A wealth of official data show that over the past decade the economic performance of state-owned firms has deteriorated in absolute terms and that the performance gap between private and state firms has widened. In short, state firms have become an increasing drag on China's economic growth in the sense that actual growth would have been more rapid if state firms had performed as well as private firms. This conclusion is supported by a comparison of state and private firms on several metrics—the extent of loss making, reliance on subsidies, return on assets, the ratio of debt to equity (the leverage ratio), and the burden of interest payments relative to pretax, preinterest earnings.[6] These comparisons rely primarily on official data from both the Ministry of Finance and the National Bureau of Statistics, as well as regulatory filings and disclosures of companies that are listed on the Shanghai and Shenzhen equity markets. The ministry's data are the most comprehensive since they cover the entire universe of state nonfinancial companies, including agricultural, industrial, construction, and service firms.[7] And they include state firms of all sizes, unlike data from the National Bureau of Statistics, which provides data on only larger industrial firms. Box 2.1 summarizes various metrics for measuring dispersion in economic performance.

Loss Making and Reliance on Subsidies

According to Ministry of Finance data, in 2005 half of all state firms were making losses (table 2.1). Eleven years later, the share of state firms reporting losses had declined slightly, but the magnitude of the losses of these firms had increased sevenfold, from RMB243 billion in 2005 to RMB1,950 billion in 2016. As a share of GDP these losses doubled, from 1.3 percent in 2005 to 2.6 percent in 2016. If one separates the loss-making state companies from the profitable ones, total losses of the former relative to the profits of the latter

---

5. Note that Dollar and Wei did not investigate dispersion in returns to labor across firms of different ownership types. The efficiency gains they estimate related only to the more efficient allocation of capital, not labor.

6. In accounting jargon this last metric is referred to as EBIT, earnings before interest and taxes.

7. The data are provided for what the Chinese call primary, secondary, and tertiary sectors. Tertiary consists of service firms, secondary covers industrial and construction firms, and primary consists of agricultural, forestry, animal husbandry, and fishery firms. Note that almost all primary production is carried out by household units rather than by enterprises. Assets of state firms in the primary sector account for less than 1 percent of the assets of state firms, an amount so small that this study provides no analysis of the efficiency of state primary sector firms.

Box 2.1 Metrics for judging economic performance

There are several possible metrics to judge systematically the performance of firms or an economy: the extent of loss making and reliance on subsidies; total factor productivity; labor productivity; capital productivity; or return on assets, i.e., profits per unit of assets, among others. This study focuses on return on assets for several reasons.

First, the data to calculate return on assets in China, disaggregated by ownership and sector, are readily available, and the calculation requires no assumptions beyond the veracity of the underlying official data. In contrast, estimating total factor productivity is very data intensive and typically requires many assumptions, leading to a large range of uncertainty around any point estimate.

Second, in China's current environment, labor productivity is likely to be a misleading measure of economic performance. High rates of investment for more than a decade have led to massive increases in the capital stock relative to the labor force (World Bank 2018c, 15, 19). When the capital stock per worker is rising, it is easy to generate increasing output per worker, but often this increase comes at the expense of a decline in output per unit of capital.

Third, China remains a capital-scarce economy, so its misallocation has a potentially larger negative effect on economic growth. If capital is allocated more efficiently, investment can be reduced without slowing growth, meaning that consumption and living standards can be improved at any given level of GDP.

Since the underlying subject of this study is economic growth, which is measured in value-added terms, ideally the analysis should be based on capital productivity, i.e., value-added per unit of assets, rather than profits per unit of assets. Unfortunately, China does not publish value-added data disaggregated by ownership or sector. Trends in revenue per unit of assets can be used as a proxy for trends in value added, if the ratio of value added to revenue is stable. Broadly speaking, these trends confirm the pattern shown in changes in return on assets, giving us confidence, for example, that the decline in the return on assets of state companies shown in figure 2.2 reflects a declining contribution of these firms to China's economic growth. In short, return on assets, an accounting measure of profitability, is a reasonable proxy for differences in capital productivity.

rose over time. As shown in the last column of the table, by 2016 this ratio had more than doubled compared with 2005 (Ministry of Finance 2015, 374; 2017b, 369).

The rapid rise between 2005 and 2016 in the absolute size of financial losses of state firms combined with a slightly decreased share of loss-making state firms strongly suggests that a large subset of state firms is losing ever

Table 2.1 Losses of state firms, 2005–16

		Losses		
Year	Loss-making share (percent)	Amount (billions of renminbi)	As a share of GDP (percent)	As a share of profits of profitable firms (percent)
2005	49.9	242.6	1.3	20.2
2006	46.6	350.8	1.6	22.3
2007	43.5	377.9	1.4	17.8
2008	43.2	652.8	2.0	32.9
2009	41.4	537.7	1.5	25.6
2010	40.0	628.7	1.5	22.7
2011	40.4	921.9	1.9	27.2
2012	41.1	1,150.9	2.1	32.2
2013	41.6	1,257.4	2.1	33.0
2014	41.9	1,452.5	2.3	35.5
2015	43.0	1,731.1	2.5	40.9
2016	43.1	1,950.2	2.6	43.3

Sources: Ministry of Finance (2015, 374; 2016a, 378; 2017b, 369); National Bureau of Statistics of China, data.stats.gov.cn; National Bureau of Statistics of China via Wind Financial Information.

larger amounts of money. If this were not the case, one would have expected the sevenfold increase in the magnitude of losses to be the result of a larger share of state firms losing money. However, the increase in the losses of the money-losing firms explains only about half of the decline in the return on assets of state companies between 2005 and 2016. The other half is due to the declining returns of profitable companies.[8]

It is important to note that the data from the Ministry of Finance, just summarized, understate the losses of loss-making state firms and overstate the profits of profitable state firms. As explained in appendix B, most listed firms receive explicit, direct subsidies from the state. Some of these firms are profitable before receiving subsidies, some are profitable only after receiving subsidies, and some continue making losses after receiving subsidies. Ministry

---

8. Based on data on the profits and assets of all state-owned companies reported by the Ministry of Finance, the return on assets of state companies fell by 2.3 percentage points, from 3.9 percent in 2005 to 1.6 percent in 2016. If the absolute losses of loss-making firms had remained unchanged after 2005, the return on assets of state companies would have fallen to only 2.8 percent. So, 1.1 percentage points of the overall decline was due to declining profitability of profitable firms and 1.2 percentage points of the overall decline was the result of the rising losses of loss-making firms.

of Finance data on the losses attributable to loss-making enterprises are understated because a portion of the direct subsidies received by firms in the second group and the entire amount of direct subsidies received by firms in the third group reduce the losses firms report to the Ministry of Finance. Similarly, ministry data on profits of profitable firms are overstated because they include all the subsidies received by firms in the first group and a portion of the subsidies received by firms in the second group.

There is no reason to believe that unlisted state firms are less successful than listed firms in qualifying for state subsidies.[9] The universe of listed state companies likely is broadly representative of all state companies, meaning profits of profitable state companies are overstated by about 10 percent and losses of loss-making state enterprises are understated by about 7 percent. That means that in 2016 the true losses of loss-making state companies were equal to half of the true profits of profitable state companies, rather than the two-fifths share indicated by Ministry of Finance data.

The ministry data just analyzed cover only state firms, but the National Bureau of Statistics provides data on losses of both state and private industrial firms.[10] While these data cover only larger industrial firms, the disaggregation of the data by type of ownership makes interesting comparisons possible. In 2016, 12 percent of all the firms included in this dataset were in the red, racking up losses of RMB817 billion. State firms made an outsized contribution to these losses. More than a quarter of state firms lost money, twice the overall share of loss-making firms among all industrial companies. And while these state firms accounted for only a fifth of the output of all industrial firms, they accounted for almost 60 percent of the losses across all forms of ownership. In contrast, less than 10 percent of private industrial firms were making losses. And although private firms accounted for more than a third of the

---

9. One might argue that since the financial performance of the broader universe of state firms is weaker than that of listed state companies that the extent of subsidies to the former would be relatively larger than the latter. However, as argued in appendix B, subsidies are not primarily to cover financial losses. Rather, they are distributed to firms that are responsive to state policy priorities.

10. Due to the peculiar organization of the data on financial losses of industrial enterprises by the National Bureau of Statistics, the coverage of private firms includes registered private firms but excludes limited liability and shareholding limited companies in which the sole, dominant, or controlling shareholder is private. On the other hand, the coverage of state firms includes both traditional state-owned firms, as well as limited liability companies in which the state is the sole, dominant, or controlling shareholder. In the industrial sector registered private companies account for about four-fifths of all private firms. For further analysis, see footnote 17 in this chapter.

output of all industrial firms, losses of unprofitable private firms accounted for only 10 percent of the losses of all industrial firms.[11] In other words, state industrial firms in 2016 were two-and-a-half times more likely than private industrial firms to be unprofitable and, relative to their output, aggregate losses of these state firms were ten times the losses of private companies.[12]

Data from the National Bureau of Statistics on losses of industrial firms allow us to make one other observation on the distribution of losses of state-owned firms: The problem of loss-making state firms is not primarily in the universe of above-scale state industrial enterprises. The losses of above-scale state industrial enterprises in 2016 were RMB499.3 billion, only a quarter of total state enterprise losses of RMB1,950.2 billion in the same year.[13] Thus three-quarters of the losses of state firms in 2016 were generated by below-scale state industrial firms and state firms in the service sector.

Return on Assets

A third metric, in addition to the extent of loss making and the degree of reliance on subsidies from the state, for judging the economic performance of companies is their return on assets, i.e., pretax profits divided by assets. The most comprehensive data come from the Ministry of Finance and cover all state nonfinancial firms, regardless of sector or size. On the return on assets measure, the efficiency of state firms was rising in all sectors in the early part of the 2000s, with average returns reaching a peak of 5 percent in 2007, just prior to the global financial crisis. Since then, returns have fallen relentlessly to an average of only 1.6 percent by 2016.[14] As shown in figure 2.2, the absolute

---

11. National Bureau of Statistics data available on Wind Financial Information.

12. Output in this paragraph is measured by sales revenue; value-added data by ownership are not available. National Bureau of Statistics data are available on Wind Financial Information.

13. Data on 2015 losses of above-scale state industrial firms are from Wind Financial Information.

14. Returns here, and elsewhere in this study, are calculated as pretax profits divided by assets. Alternatively, one may want to measure returns as profits plus interest expenses divided by assets. That approach implicitly treats pretax profits as the return on equity and interest expenditure as the return on debt, with the sum representing the return on invested capital, financed by either equity or debt. This alternative calculation leads to a higher measure of return for all state enterprises in China, 6.4 percent in 2007. But on this measure returns fell to 2.7 percent by 2016, proportionately only slightly less than the fall from 5.0 percent to 1.6 percent. So using the alternative measure of returns would not significantly change the conclusions drawn in this study.

Figure 2.2 Return on assets of state-owned enterprises by sector, 2003–16

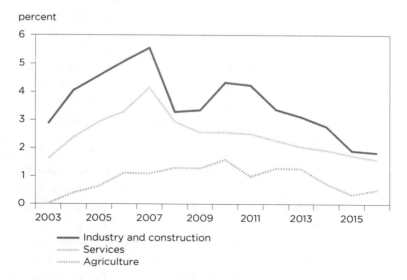

percent

Sources: Ministry of Finance (2017b, 379, 383); Wind Financial Information.

decline was greatest for state industrial and construction firms, but the return on assets of state service sector firms also fell.[15]

Again, since a portion of the profits of state firms is due to subsidies, these data on return on assets overstate the financial performance of state firms. Two points are explained in more detail in appendix B. First, the official data shown in figure 2.2 overstate the return on assets of state companies. In 2015, for example, the true return, i.e., not including the value of explicit, direct subsidies embedded in reported firm profits, was 1.4 percent, not the reported 1.8 percent. Second, the degree of overstatement of profits and thus return on assets has been increasing over time, so the pace of decline in the return on assets of state companies is understated in the figure.

The extraordinarily low average return on assets of state companies is consistent with Ministry of Finance data showing that more than 40 percent of state enterprises were losing money in 2016, i.e., more than two-fifths of all state firms were unable to fully cover their cost of capital. The latter is the average interest rate in 2016 on bank loans to nonfinancial corporations,

---

15. Revenues, a proxy for value added, per unit of output of state firms declined by almost half over the same period, confirming the increasing drag of state firms on China's economic growth since the global financial crisis.

weighted across all maturities, of 5.54 percent (People's Bank of China Monetary Policy Analysis Small Group 2017, 6). The calculation of an average return on assets is based on profits after the payment of interest expense. So a positive average return on assets in 2015 means that, on average, state firms were covering their cost of capital.

But one needs to consider the variance in the performance of individual firms in the universe of state firms. Disaggregated data for the universe of listed state companies show that between 2006 and 2011 the leverage ratio significantly increased at the tail end of the distribution (Chivakul and Lam 2015). This observation is consistent with a distribution of returns that is not normal. As noted above, in the aggregate data from the Ministry of Finance, as average returns have fallen, the share of state firms losing money has not increased, but the magnitude of losses has risen both in absolute terms and relative to GDP, i.e., larger losses are being generated by the two-fifths of firms that are making losses. Thus, to the extent that these losses are covered by increased borrowing, for the larger universe of state-owned firms the leverage ratio must be increasing especially rapidly at the tail end of the distribution.

The best data to compare the relative performance of state and private firms based on return on assets are in industry. Figure 2.3 shows that the return on assets of state-owned industrial firms has always lagged that of private firms.[16] The gap was greatly reduced by the market-oriented reforms of the second half of the 1990s, which led to the closure or privatization of many least efficient state firms, and by major cuts in tariffs and nontariff barriers that were a key part of China's negotiations to enter the World Trade Organization, which increased competition in the domestic economy. But from the middle of the last decade, as the productivity gains generated by these earlier reform initiatives waned and, as noted in chapter 1, the leadership of President Hu Jintao and Premier Wen Jiabao took few potentially offsetting additional

---

16. Throughout this study the return on assets for state industrial companies is based on the profits and assets of state industrial companies broadly defined, i.e., including traditional state industrial companies as well as state-controlled shareholding industrial companies (see footnote 11, chapter 1). The return on assets of private companies is based on the profits and assets of registered private companies only. The statistical authorities have not published systematic data on the profits and assets of limited liability companies and shareholding limited companies that are privately controlled. In 2017 registered private companies accounted for 60 percent of the combined profits of registered private companies and privately controlled limited liability and shareholding limited companies. Lardy (2014, 97ff) provides additional analysis of why the performance of registered private companies is a reasonable proxy for the broader universe of private firms.

Figure 2.3   Return on assets of state and private industrial enterprises, 1996–2016

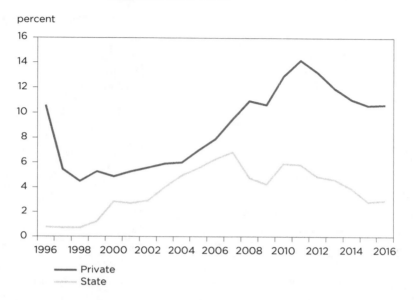

percent

Sources: National Bureau of Statistics of China (2017e, 424–25, 430–31); National Bureau of Statistics of China, data.stats.gov.cn (accessed on September 5, 2017).

economic reform measures, the gap began to grow, and it exploded during and after the global financial crisis, reaching 3.5:1 by 2016.[17]

The pattern shown in figure 2.3 is broadly mirrored by data on revenue per unit of assets of state and private industrial firms. For state firms this metric, which is a proxy for value added per unit of assets, declined by a little more than half between 2007 and 2016. That decline is a bit more than the decline in return on assets over the same period. For private firms, revenue per unit of assets rose steadily from 2007 to a peak in 2011 and then declined to 2016 but at the endpoint was higher than in 2017, a pattern like the return on assets trajectory for private firms shown in figure 2.3. This supports the judgment that the steadily weakening performance of state-owned firms is an important factor explaining China's slowing economic growth since the global financial crisis.

---

17. The figure almost certainly overstates the performance of state-owned industrial companies since it is limited to the universe of so-called above-scale firms, which in recent years has meant annual sales of more than RMB20 million.

Table 2.2   Return on assets of state and private service sector firms, 2008 (percent)

Sector	State	Nonstate	Private-registered
Wholesale and retail trade	8.7	7.9	9.5
Hotels and catering services	0.6	4.6	7.1
Information transmission, software, and information technology	8.4	12.6	n.a.
Leasing and business services	1.4	3.9	n.a.
Scientific research, technical services, and geological prospecting	4.7	2.5	n.a.
Management of water conservancy, environment, and public facilities	0.7	6.6	n.a.
Household services and other services	2.9	17.7	n.a.
Education	8.1	16.0	n.a.
Health, social security, and social welfare	10.4	10.3	n.a.
Culture, sports, and entertainment	5.1	7.6	n.a.
Total	**3.4**	**6.6**	**8.3**

n.a. = not available

Sources: National Bureau of Statistics of China (2010b, www.stats.gov.cn/tjsj/pcsj); author's calculations.

There are no aggregate time series data for private service sector firms that could be used to compare with the return on assets of state service companies, shown in figure 2.2. Instead, one must look at individual components of the service sector for data for both state and private firms, typically only for a single year. China's 2008 national economic census fortunately did provide relevant information on 10 of the 14 components of the service sector.[18] In the most disaggregated form the census provided information on the assets and profits of state firms and nonstate firms. The universe of nonstate firms includes collective and foreign firms, but private firms dominate this universe, so the returns of nonstate firms may be taken as a reasonable proxy for the returns of private firms. At a much less disaggregated level the census also provided evidence on the profits and assets of registered private firms. These data, summarized in table 2.2, show that the average return on assets of state firms in 10 of the 14 components of the service sector was 3.4 percent compared with

---

18. The 2008 census did not provide data on the following components of the service sector: transportation, storage, and post; financial intermediation; real estate; and public management, social security, and social organization.

6.6 percent for nonstate firms and 8.3 percent for registered private firms.[19] Unfortunately, the next national economic census in 2013 provided data on assets and revenues of state and private service sector companies but did not include any data on profits.

Credit, Leverage, and Interest Burden

The deteriorating performance of state firms since the global financial crisis, as measured by the mounting financial losses and declining return on assets, is closely related to the large increase in domestic credit relative to GDP in recent years and the associated accumulation of risks in China's financial sector. The credit (to the government, households, and nonfinancial corporations) to GDP ratio after 2011 rise by about 60 percentage points to reach 234 percent at the end of 2016, much higher than in countries at similar levels of economic development and comparable to countries that have experienced painful deleveraging (IMF 2017b, 17, 23). As shown in figure 2.4, credit to nonfinancial corporations rose from 120 percent of GDP in 2009 to 166 percent by the end of 2016. Thus, nonfinancial corporations have accounted for the lion's share of the 60 percentage point increase in aggregate credit over the same years. At the end of 2016 China had "the most leveraged corporate sector in the world."[20] The IMF (2017b, 16) identifies the outsized role of state firms in the sharp increase in the debt of China's nonfinancial corporates relative to GDP. It estimates that borrowing by state firms accounted for three-quarters of the rise in this ratio between 2008 and 2016.

In addition to looking at the ratio of credit to GDP of nonfinancial corporations, it is useful to examine the leverage ratio of borrowers, i.e., the ratio of liabilities to equity, the latter being equal to total assets minus total liabilities, i.e., net worth or equity. This approach recognizes that if a firm is worth more, i.e., has more equity, other things being equal, it is likely to be a better credit risk. If that is the case, by lending increased amounts to such a firm, a lender is not necessarily assuming greater risk. Figure 2.5 shows that the leverage ratio for all industrial firms changed little between the early 2000s and 2013 and has since declined somewhat. The ending ratio in 2016 was below the level in

---

19. The returns of nonstate service enterprises are likely to be a reasonable proxy for the returns of private service enterprises. In addition to private firms, nonstate firms would include collective and foreign firms. But these other forms of ownership account for a very small portion of the assets of service sector nonstate firms.

20. "China's Balancing Act on Debt Is Becoming Trickier," *Financial Times*, November 17, 2017, 10.

Figure 2.4 Nonfinancial corporate credit, 2006Q1–2017Q3

percent of GDP

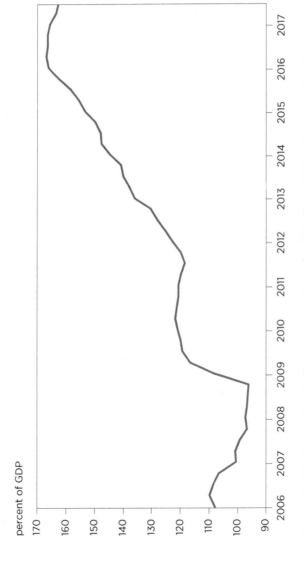

Source: Bank for International Settlements, www.bis.org/statistics/totcredit.htm (last updated on September 17, 2017).

Figure 2.5 Leverage ratio of industrial companies by ownership, 1998–2016

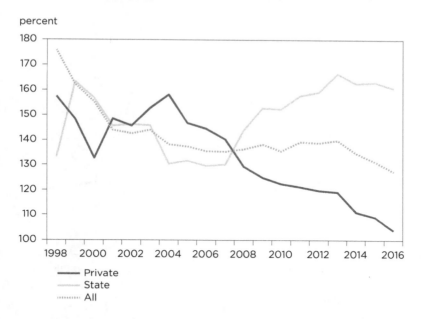

Sources: National Bureau of Statistics of China, data.stats.gov.cn (accessed on March 14, 2018); National Bureau of Statistics of China via Wind Financial Information (accessed on August 1, 2018).

2007–08. Thus, for the broad universe of Chinese industrial firms the leverage ratio metric has not deteriorated since the global financial crisis.

The figure also reveals that the average leverage ratio of state industrial firms rose sharply between 2007 and 2013 and then moderated slightly. In contrast, the average leverage ratio of private industrial firms has fallen continuously for more than a decade. Consequently, the leverage ratio of state industrial firms is now half again as high as that of private firms, a sharp change from 2007, when the leverage ratio of both types of firms was equal.

In addition to analyzing trends in the leverage ratio, one can examine the share of pretax, preinterest earnings of industrial firms that is absorbed by interest payments (figure 2.6). This is simply the inverse of the interest coverage ratio, one of the most common metrics of creditworthiness. The higher the ratio, the more likely that in a downturn a firm would be unable to repay its lenders. The trend is very similar to that of the average leverage ratio: rising sharply for state firms since the global financial crisis while gradually declining for more than a decade for private firms. The average share of pretax, preinterest income of state companies absorbed by interest payments more than doubled from 15 percent in 2006 to more than 30 percent in 2015 before

Figure 2.6 Interest payments of industrial firms as a share of pretax profits, 2006–16

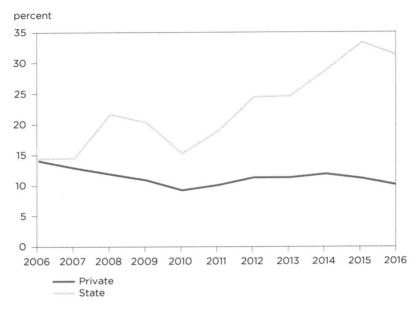

percent

Sources: National Bureau of Statistics of China, data.stats.gov.cn (accessed on March 14, 2018); National Bureau of Statistics of China via Wind Financial Information (accessed on August 1, 2018).

falling slightly in 2016. The rising trend reflects the combination of rapidly rising liabilities, mostly bank loans, and a decline in the return on assets of these firms. In short, state firms on average became less and less creditworthy after the global financial crisis.

While both state and private firms rely on borrowing from banks and credit markets to finance part of their investment, the data on leverage ratios and the share of operating earnings absorbed by interest payments confirm the view that on average private industrial firms have invested retained earnings and borrowed funds in projects that have generated relatively high returns, allowing these firms to amortize their debt, thus increasing their assets relative to their liabilities and reducing both their leverage ratio and the share of pretax, preinterest income devoted to paying interest. In contrast, on average, state firms have used more modest retained earnings and a larger amount of borrowed funds to invest in projects that on average generate relatively low returns, impairing their ability to amortize their debt. As this cycle continues, many of these state firms use newly borrowed funds to pay the interest on previous loans, which inevitably increases their liabilities faster than their assets and raises their leverage ratios and the burden of interest payments relative to their operating income.

A detailed analysis of the data on about 2,500 Chinese companies listed on the Shanghai, Shenzhen, and Hong Kong stock markets for the years 2003–13 extends the analysis of trends in leverage across different types of ownership to a universe that includes service sector firms (Chivakul and Lam 2015).[21] Over this period, the median leverage ratio of private listed companies declined steadily from about 125 percent in 2006 to 55 percent in 2013 while the median leverage of listed state companies remained flat at about 110 percent.[22] Thus, in this sample of firms, which includes a large number of service sector firms, the leverage of state companies is twice that of private companies, a much larger gap than that for state and private industrial companies, shown in figure 2.5. Moreover, while the median leverage of listed state companies has been relatively flat since 2006, the leverage ratio of these firms has increased significantly at the tail end of the distribution at the 75th and 90th percentiles, driven largely by increased leverage of state firms in real estate and construction (Chivakul and Lam 2015, 7).

The same study of listed firms found that considering firm liquidity, profitability, and solvency, the balance sheets of private firms improved while those of state-owned enterprises deteriorated over the decade ending in 2013. Not surprisingly, given these trends, state firms are more vulnerable to shocks, such as rising interest rates or a decline in revenue from the real estate and construction sectors. Under various scenarios analyzed, debt at risk, i.e., the amount of loans and bonds of firms with earnings (prior to interest and taxes) less than interest expense, rises sharply, with most of the increase accounted for by state companies (Chivakul and Lam 2015).

Explaining the Weaker Performance of State Firms

The large and growing gap in the economic and financial performance of private and state firms reflects the superior management of the former and the failure of banks, almost entirely state-owned, to impose hard budget constraints on money-losing state-owned enterprises. Private firms attempt to maximize profits and returns on assets while managers of many state companies appear to be asset maximizers, borrowing ever larger amounts to expand

---

21. The study excluded firms classified in the financial industry.

22. These numbers suggest that the financial performance of listed companies has been better than that of all firms. The leverage ratio of listed private companies has declined more than that of all private companies and the leverage ratio of listed state companies has remained flat while that of all state companies has risen significantly.

their businesses even if the returns do not cover the cost of capital. But alternative, more benign explanations abound. Most of them imply that state firms may be just as efficient as private firms but that they face different constraints that lead to predictably lower returns on capital. Some of the explanations suggest that there is little or no possibility that China's economic growth could be boosted if the returns of state firms converged toward the level of private firms. In evaluating these explanations, it is essential to distinguish between those that may explain the difference in the return on assets in state firms compared with private firms and those that may explain the decade-long decline in the return on assets of state firms relative to private firms.

First, state firms may face a lower cost of capital. So, if both private and state firms are successful profit maximizers, one should expect the return on assets of state firms to be lower. Second, the different product mix of state and private firms could be contributing to their divergent performance. In any economy during a cyclical decline in economic growth, the demand for capital goods typically moderates much more than the demand for consumer goods. If state firms primarily produce the former while private firms primarily produce the latter, one would expect the economic performance of state firms to deteriorate relative to that of private firms when growth slows. Similarly, state firms may be more exposed to fluctuations in international commodity prices than private firms, which could contribute to the performance gap. Third, the underlying efficiency of state and private firms may be similar, but this similarity may be masked because state firms provide a much broader range of services to their workers than their private firm counterparts, depressing their reported profitability. Fourth, underperformance of state firms relative to private firms is particularly acute in services. Perhaps the characteristics of the service sector are an important factor in explaining the weaker performance of state firms.

Does the Lower Cost of Capital Explain the Low Returns of State Companies?

The first alternative explanation is that state firms are just as motivated to make profits and just as effective at maximizing profits as private firms and that, like private firms, they employ capital up to the point where the marginal returns are equal to the marginal cost of capital, i.e., the interest rate they pay on loans. According to this view, the lower returns of state firms reflect their preferential access to capital, i.e., an interest rate lower than what private firms pay (Hsieh and Song 2015). If state firms can access funds at a much lower cost than private firms, it will be efficient for them to employ more capital, up to the point where the returns are equal to their lower marginal cost of capital.

One must acknowledge that banks in all economies typically do not lend to small private firms with little or no collateral and a short or nonexistent record of profitability. These small, private firms are financed initially by borrowing from family and friends or from the informal credit market, where interest rates are likely to be quite high. One example is Chinese microfinance firms that extend loans to individuals and small, individual private companies, which until 2011 were not allowed to have more than seven nonfamily employees. The regulator allows microfinance firms to charge up to four times the central bank's benchmark interest rates for loans of various maturities. The average interest rate on loans from microfinance companies in Zhejiang, a province with a vibrant private sector, for example, was 17.4 and 20.8 percent in 2010 and 2011, respectively. These rates were about 3.5 times the then prevailing benchmark rate on loans of up to 6 months, which is a typical maturity on a loan from a microfinance company (China Banking Society 2011, 372, 559; 2012, 414, 600). So large state firms undoubtedly borrow at rates lower than small private startups.

If we focus on firms that have been able to access the formal bank credit market, the most systematic evidence only partially supports the view that state firms have preferential access to capital, reflected in lower ex ante interest rates than faced by private firms. Two comprehensive surveys, one in 2004–05 and another in 2011, both showed that state firms enjoyed only a modest interest rate advantage relative to private firms, on the order of three-tenths of a percentage point. The first was a joint survey undertaken by the People's Bank of China and the International Finance Corporation (an arm of the World Bank Group) of 100 financial institutions in 2004–05. It found that these financial institutions, on average, charged private firms 5.96 percent while state firms paid on average 5.67 percent (IFC 2007, 57). The 2011 survey, by a group of Chinese institutions, found that private firms paid 7.8 percent, only slightly above the average bank lending rate of 7.5 percent (Lardy 2014, 108). Assuming that state firm managers are rational profit maximizers, the somewhat lower interest rates paid by state borrowers in 2004–05 could explain a proportion of the then small difference of 1.25 percentage points in the return on assets of state and private industrial firms. But in 2011, when the gap in the return on assets had expanded to more than 8 percentage points, the slightly lower ex ante cost of capital of state firms could explain only a small portion of the gap.

However, for the large subset of state firms that are losing money and likely to receive state subsidies to offset their losses or have their loans partially or wholly forgiven, the ex ante interest rates reported for state firm borrowers in the two surveys just summarized may not be relevant. Managers of these firms may expand their firms well past the point at which the marginal returns their firms can generate are just equal to the cost of capital. However, while this strategy may be rational from the point of view of an enterprise manager, it likely is far from optimal from a broader perspective. Since loss-making firms are unable to cover the real cost of capital, they are a net drain on society's resources.

While subsidies or loan forgiveness may partly explain the lower returns of state companies, it seems less likely that the trends in the cost of capital these firms face can explain the trends in their return on assets. Compare the time pattern of the benchmark one-year interest rate shown in figure 2.7 with trends in the return on assets of state companies shown in figure 2.2. Bank lending interest rates were flat when the average return on assets of state firms was rising from the early 2000s through 2007 and rates fell only slightly after the global financial crisis, when the return on assets of state firms fell persistently. Thus, in both periods there is little support for the hypothesis that trends in the return on assets of state firms are explained by trends in the cost of capital.

Does the Product Mix of State Companies Explain Their Underperformance?

A second potential explanation of the growing gap between private and state industrial firms focuses on the different product mix of state and private firms. In an economic slowdown, like China experienced from 2008 through 2016, the demand for capital goods, such as steel and machinery, typically slows more than the demand for consumer goods, such as food and clothing. If state firms predominate in industries like steel, while private firms predominate in the production of consumer goods, then during an economic slowdown the average return of state firms would be expected to fall relative to returns of private firms. Jon Anderson has persistently asserted this view, arguing that China does not really have a "state-enterprise problem, rather it's a heavy industrial problem" (Anderson 2017, 7). Some empirical studies on this issue, however, show that state firms underperform their private peers within the same industry or sector (IMF 2017b, 26; Gatley 2017, 31).

Closely related to this argument, trends in global commodity prices will affect profitability in industries producing oil and gas, coal, and other commodities. If state firms dominate in these industries, returns of the broader universe of state firms will be correlated with global commodity prices, independent of the efficiency of the operations of these firms. The international price of crude oil fell from an average of over $100 per barrel from mid-2013 to mid-2014 to less than $30 by the end of 2015 and then recovered to the

Figure 2.7   Benchmark interest rate on one-year loans, January 1990–November 2017

percent

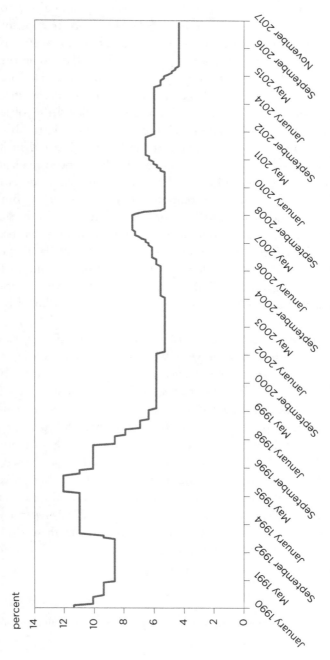

Sources: People's Bank of China, www.pbc.gov.cn/zhengcehuobisi/125207/125213/125440/125838/125888/index.html (accessed on December 15, 2017); Wind Financial Information.

mid-$40s by mid-year 2016 through mid-year 2017.[23] Since the domestic price of crude oil in China is closely tied to the international price and since state firms account for about 85 percent of output of the upstream oil and gas industry, the profits of state oil and gas companies plummeted as prices fell. These firms earned RMB335 billion in 2013 but turned in a loss of RMB75 billion by 2016 (National Bureau of Statistics of China 2014, 408–10; 2017e, 420–23). If profits in the state oil and gas industry in 2016 had remained at the elevated level of 2013, the return on assets of all state industrial firms in 2016 would have been 3.9 percent rather than the 3.0 percent reflected in figure 2.3.

To shed further light on the product mix explanation, let's look at the steel industry, a prime exemplar of a capital-intensive, heavy industry. It's useful to note that state firms are far less dominant in heavy industry than frequently assumed. Yes, state firms continue to monopolize both upstream oil and gas, as well as electric power generation and distribution, and play a somewhat larger role than private firms in a few components of heavy industry. But in some important heavy industries state firms are not so dominant. In the steel industry, for example, the share of output produced by state firms has been falling throughout the reform period, and on the eve of the global financial crisis in 2007 these firms accounted for only 45 percent of steel output (National Bureau of Statistics of China 2008, 486–89, 496–99).[24] Most of the balance was produced by private firms and a small share was contributed by foreign-owned firms.

Prior to the global financial crisis, returns of state steel firms exceeded those of private firms in some years while in other years the opposite was true, so the multiyear average returns were roughly equal across both state and private steel firms. But the relative performance of state steel firms declined dramatically as the global financial crisis unfolded. As shown in figure 2.8, the returns of private and state firms were both 5.6 percent in 2006, but subsequently the returns of private firms rose strongly to more than 10 percent in 2010 and 2011, while the returns of state firms collapsed to under 2 percent. State firms began to lose money in 2012, roughly broke even in 2013–14, incurred major losses in 2015, and recovered to almost breakeven in 2016. The cumulative net losses of state steel firms in 2012–16 were RMB110 billion. The returns of private steel firms declined from their 2011 peak of 10.6 percent but remained well into profitable territory. What accounts for the dramatic divergence in performance?

---

23. Prices quoted are for Brent crude from US Energy Information Administration.

24. Measured by the value of sales, not tons of output.

Figure 2.8   Return on assets of steel industry by ownership, 2000–16

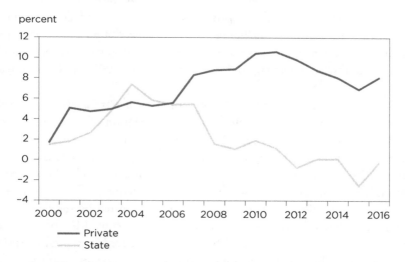

percent

Sources: National Bureau of Statistics of China (2017e, 420–23, 426–29); National Bureau of Statistics of China, data.stats.gov.cn (accessed on March 14, 2018).

In the decade to 2010 apparent domestic steel consumption in China exploded, from about 140 million metric tons to 775 million metric tons, an annual growth averaging 19 percent.[25] In the next six years, apparent steel demand grew at an average annual rate of only 5 percent. Most of the growth was in 2011–12, and it was essentially flat in 2013–16. As the pace of domestic steel demand softened, private firms adjusted relatively successfully to rapidly changing market conditions. Declining profits followed by years of losses meant that investment by state-owned steel firms plummeted after 2008, while private firms invested increasing amounts in modernizing their facilities, improving product quality, and lowering costs.[26] By 2015, in the face of persistently weak domestic demand, the returns of private steel firms had fallen to 6.9 percent, a few percentage points below their peak returns of 10.6

---

25. To measure true annual domestic consumption of steel requires data on changes in inventories. Absent those data, I rely on apparent steel consumption, which is equal to production minus net exports.

26. State steel firms invested more than twice as much as private firms in 2007 and 2008. By 2013 state firm investment was half the level of 2008 while private firm investment more than tripled and was three times the level of investment of state steel firms (Wind Financial Information).

percent in 2011, but were miles ahead of state steel companies, where losses of RMB870 billion had driven returns to an all-time low of −2.5 percent.

The superior performance of private steel firms since the global financial crisis is also reflected in the further decline in the share of output of state steel companies to 26 percent in 2016, less than half the share of private firms and a decline of almost 20 percentage points compared with 2007 (National Bureau of Statistics of China 2017e, 414–17, 420–23).

Thus, part of the decline in the performance of state relative to private industrial firms in 2013–16 is due to the concentration of state firms in oil and gas extraction, where the declining global crude oil price depressed profits. But the more general hypothesis that the declining return on assets of state firms relative to private players is due to the preponderant role of the former in capital-intensive industries, which experience a relatively sharper decline in demand as economic growth slows, is not well supported by the data. First, state firms no longer dominate some of China's most capital-intensive industries. A general decline in demand for output produced in capital-intensive industries where both state and private firms produce a significant share of output would depress the return on industrial assets in both state and private firms. It would thus not be a major contributor to the rapidly declining relative performance of the larger universe of state-owned firms compared with private firms since the global financial crisis. This is illustrated in the steel industry, where returns rose for both state and private firms in 2016 as Chinese policy began to reduce excess supply in the industry and prices began to rise. Initial evidence suggests that this trend strengthened in 2017 when profits in above-scale plants in the industry rose by 177 percent (National Bureau of Statistics of China 2018c).[27] But the large gap in the return on assets of state and private steel firms persisted, at least through 2016.

Second, private firms in steel, a capital-intensive industry, seem to have adjusted to rapidly changing market conditions more nimbly than their state firm competitors. Further research on other capital-intensive industries, where both state and private firms are major players, would shed light on whether the steel industry is an exception or reflects a more general pattern.

---

27. This large increase in profits in the steel industry in 2017 is not reflected in the figure because at the time of this writing profit data for the steel industry disaggregated by ownership were not available.

Do Excessive Social Burdens Explain the Weaker Performance of State Companies?

The third alternative explanation of the relative underperformance of state companies is that these firms have significant social responsibilities that are funded from their operating revenue, thus reducing their reported profits and contributing a large portion of the productivity gap between state and private firms (IMF 2017a, 15). Evidence on the large magnitude of these burdens in the mid-1990s, prior to the reforms of state-owned enterprises orchestrated by Premier Zhu Rongji, is abundant. At that time, for example, state firms operated more than 18,000 schools employing 600,000 teachers and staff and built and paid the operating costs of thousands of hospitals that accounted for one-third of all hospital beds in China. One survey showed that these social expenditures absorbed about 8 percent of the revenues of profitable state-owned firms (Lardy 1998, 51).

In addition, many state companies built housing for their workers and retirees, which were usually rented at a highly subsidized rate and thus generated funds insufficient to cover even the cost of building maintenance. Construction costs, also borne by state organizations, including state enterprises, were considerable since state organizations annually had to build 50 to 60 percent of all new urban housing between 1985 and 1995, pushing up the stock of state-owned residential housing from 116 million square meters in 1985 to 177 million square meters in 1995 (Lardy 1998, 50–51).

In the absence of a social security system, in which pension contributions are pooled and retirement benefits paid to retirees by a government agency, state-owned firms were also directly responsible for supporting their retired workers. Payments to retirees were part of every state firm's overall wage bill. Since many state firms were established and expanded rapidly in the 1950s, by the beginning of the reform era the ratio of retirees to current employees in many state enterprises was rising, imposing an increasing financial burden. Private firms, which began emerging in the 1980s and especially the 1990s, typically had no retirees and thus had an inherent operating cost advantage over state firms that had operated in many cases for decades.

Finally, a fourth major component of the social burdens of state enterprises was avoiding layoffs to sustain high levels of employment. One survey in the mid-1990s found that more than half of all state firms had excess employees, with a third of the firms putting the share of redundant workers at more than a fifth (Lardy 1998, 50).

The cumulative burden of these social responsibilities undoubtedly contributed to the very weak financial performance of state firms prior to their downsizing in the late 1990s.

The magnitude of these burdens on state firms two decades later is considerably less. State firms began selling off their housing stock to employees on a small-scale, trial basis as early as 1982. The pace picked up in 1988, when the government announced the National Housing Reform Plan to encourage private home ownership, and accelerated further after mid-1998, when the government announced the end of the "administratively planned housing distribution system" (Lardy 2014, 149). Firms typically sold housing to their employees at below market prices, but they nonetheless gained for two reasons. First, they gained on a cash flow basis, since the sales shifted most maintenance costs to the new owners. Second, state firms were relieved of the responsibility of investing in additional housing if their number of workers and retirees grew, because housing rapidly became a commodity produced mostly by private firms and sold through the market.

The government also began to relieve state enterprises of their healthcare, education, and other social responsibilities as the economic reforms of Premier Zhu Rongji unfolded in the second half of the 1990s. For example, while state firms continued to run many schools, they received increasing levels of financial support for these activities directly from the state budget. By 2013 state enterprises were spending only RMB4.8 billion of their own operating revenue on running educational institutions, less than a fifth of the operating costs of the schools they administered (Ministry of Education Finance Office and National Bureau of Statistics Social, Scientific, and Cultural Affairs Statistical Office 2014, 16–17). This amount is vanishingly small because it had no material effect on either the profits of profitable firms or the losses of money-losing firms.[28] And in mid-2017 several government departments jointly announced that the balance of the education and healthcare burdens on state enterprises would be transferred entirely to local governments by the end of 2018. The exception was vocational schools, which would continue to be run by state enterprises, presumably because most of students in these schools are being trained for employment within these enterprises (SASAC et al. 2017). But the state enterprises spent under RMB1 billion on vocational education in 2013.

The excess retirement burden on state firms began to be eroded in the mid-1980s, when China introduced payroll taxes in state-owned firms to support pension payments and adopted municipal pension pools all over China

---

28. If profitable state firms had entirely borne the burden of these educational outlays of RMB4.8 billion, it would have represented only 0.1 percent of their reported profits. If money-losing state firms had entirely borne the burden, it would have represented only 0.4 percent of their reported losses.

(World Bank 1996). This change meant that the retirement burden on any state firm was primarily a function of the firm's wage bill for current workers and thus was independent of the number retirees.[29] By the early 1990s more than three-quarters of employees in state enterprises participated in pension pools.

Over time three additional developments more widely distributed the direct burden on state firms of supporting their own retired workers, reducing the competitive disadvantage of older, mostly state-owned firms versus newer, predominantly private firms. First, pooling was done at higher administrative levels. By the mid-1990s, for example, 9 of 32 provincial-level administrative units were experimenting with some form of pooling (World Bank 1997, 21). This number gradually expanded and by the end of 2017 the Ministry of Human Resources and Social Security (2017a) said that unification of the social security system at the provincial level was basically complete and that the initial steps for pooling at the national level would occur in 2018. China's highest-level executive agency later confirmed this plan and announced that it would be implemented starting in July 2018 (State Council 2018a).

Second, the scope of the pension system was gradually expanded to include nonstate firms. In the late 1980s pooling was extended to collectively owned enterprises in many cities, and later foreign enterprises, joint ventures, and private firms were also included (World Bank 1997, 16). Most of these nonstate firms had few retirees, so, in what was and still is essentially a pay-as-you-go pension system, the payroll taxes earmarked for pensions paid by these firms initially went largely to pay for the pensions of retirees from state enterprises.[30]

Finally, the government began to provide direct budgetary subsidies to the pension system, largely to cover deficits in geographic areas where pension contributions fell short of pension outlays (Zhao and Xu 2001, 194). These subsidies were initially modest, about RMB5 billion in 1997, but grew rapidly, reaching RMB651 billion by 2016, an amount equivalent to almost a fourth of the income of the pension system derived from payroll taxes paid by firms and individuals (Ministry of Human Resources and Social Security 2017b, 5).

---

29. However, some pension pools charged higher contribution rates to older enterprises with a larger ratio of retirees to current employees (World Bank 1996, 33).

30. Annual revenues, including the subsidy provided through the state budget, of the combined pension schemes for urban workers and urban and rural residents only slightly exceed pension expenditures. At the end of 2016 the pension fund balance was RMB4.4 trillion, an amount sufficient to support only about 9 months of pension outlays (National Bureau of Statistics of China 2017e, 790).

In the absence of this subsidy, contribution rates in cities and provinces with a relatively large number of retirees would be higher, imposing a competitive disadvantage on firms in these areas.

In addition, the Zhu Rongji reforms of the mid- to late 1990s drastically reduced the burden on state enterprises of their mandate to maintain employment. Estimates of the number of workers who lost their jobs vary, but according to one comprehensive study, this aggressive restructuring "led to the layoffs of at least 10 million workers by 1997 and 27 million workers from 1998 to 2004, mostly from the state sector" (Cai, Park, and Zhao 2008, 176).

Do State Firms Underperform Because Services Are Different?

Finally, as noted earlier in this chapter, a large share of the financial losses of state firms occurs in the service sector. Some public services may be provided at subsidized prices, so loss making may reflect state policy. For example, except in Hong Kong, subway systems globally make losses. China is no exception: Most individual lines reportedly lose money. But urban mass transit systems generate large positive externalities, reflected in reduced pollution, less congestion, and so forth. So subsidies to encourage the use of mass transit may be economically and socially rational, even though on a direct financial basis the companies providing the services are making losses. However, China's subway lines that have negative operating income don't necessarily report pretax losses, so it is not clear that state companies operating subway systems or providing other public services are dragging down the reported returns on assets of state service sector firms. In 2010, for example, the Shenzhen Metro Group had operating losses of about RMB200 million. But, with a subsidy of RMB830 million from the government, the group, following standard enterprise accounting practices that treat subsidies as a revenue, reported a pretax profit of RMB630 million.[31] Similarly, the Beijing municipal government provided subway subsidies totaling RMB22 billion in the six years from 2007 to 2013, drastically reducing reported pretax losses or perhaps leading to a position of pretax profitability.[32]

Moreover, as shown in table 2.2, state enterprises greatly underperform in some components of services where it is difficult to make a case for price subsidies. In 2008, private hotels and restaurants, for example, earned returns

---

31. Ye Jingyu, "Why Subways Suffer Losses," *Economic Observer*, August 13, 2012, www.eeo.com (accessed on August 14, 2012) [discontinued as of October 25, 2013. The site is still up but no search function is available].

32. Hu Yongqi, "Measures Will Shunt Subway Plans onto Sidings," *China Daily*, July 18, 2018, 6.

more than ten times higher than their state counterparts. State firms providing leasing and business services, which presumably should be priced on a competitive market basis, earn returns that are only one-third of nonstate providers of these services.

More generally, state firms underperform in services primarily because the state limits the issue of licenses to private firms in some components of services. In manufacturing, private firms face few entry restrictions and have substantially increased competition, in the process largely displacing inefficient state firms that previously dominated the production of a very broad range of goods. Because of this displacement, by 2015 state firms accounted for only 8 percent of all manufacturing investment (National Bureau of Statistics of China 2016b, 318–19). They had ceded almost the entire space to private firms. On the other hand, in 2015 state firms accounted for 45 percent of all investment in services. Restrictions on entry reduce competition, allowing many inefficient state services firms to survive, rather than stepping up their game to compete with more efficient private firms (National Bureau of Statistics of China 2016b, 318–21).

Real Explanations of the Weaker Performance of State Firms

The alternative explanations just described are not very convincing. The falling cost of capital cannot explain the large decline in the rate of return of state companies after the global financial crisis: Bank lending rates fell only slightly between 2007 and 2015. The downturn in global commodity prices starting in the second half of 2014 did reduce profits in the state-dominated upstream oil and gas industry, but more research would be required to test the more general product mix explanation. In one capital-intensive industry, steel, the financial performance of state companies has fallen dramatically relative to private steel firms since the global financial crisis. The various social burdens imposed on state companies have eased sharply in the past 30 years, which means the real deterioration in the economic and financial performance of state enterprises is greater than is reflected in official data. Finally, the extremely low returns of state service sector firms may primarily reflect entry restrictions on private firms in some services, rather than state underpricing of services with significant social benefits.

This takes us to what I regard as the real explanations of the underperformance of state firms vis-à-vis their private counterparts: insufficient profit maximizing behavior, including corruption, on the part of the senior management of state firms and a large misallocation of capital by Chinese financial institutions, especially banks. A detailed analysis of capital flows within large state and private group companies that control many listed subsidiaries (Ljungqvist et al. 2015) supports the former explanation. This study of 660 listed state-owned firms controlled by 211 state groups found that within-group capital allocations are significantly negatively related to investment opportunities, i.e., within groups, listed subsidiary firms with better investment opportunities experienced capital outflows to their parent, while subsidiary firms with inferior investment opportunities received inflows from their parent. In contrast, 76 private groups controlling a total of 166 private listed firms tended to allocate capital to their subsidiary firms with the best investment opportunities. The authors of the study further found that the tendency of state groups to allocate capital perversely is stronger when product market competition is weak and when the group parent has greater control over its listed subsidiaries, i.e., when external monitoring by minority private shareholders of subsidiary firms is weaker.[33]

Finally, based on the hypothesis that group chairs have an important influence on each group's internal capital allocation decisions, Ljungqvist et al. (2015) argue that the allocation of capital within state groups is perverse because it is driven by the desire of group chairs to maximize their chances of promotion, rather than maximizing profits or shareholder value. The chances of promotion, the authors of the study argue, are increased by raising productivity and avoiding layoffs at subsidiary firms within the group. But there is asymmetry in this incentive structure—productivity improvements are rewarded, but productivity impairments are mostly ignored. So avoiding layoffs at subsidiary firms becomes the primary goal of the senior management at the group level, leading to internal capital allocations that prop up larger and struggling subsidiaries within each group.

An examination of the thermal electric power generation industry, where a handful of state firms produce almost all electricity, also demonstrates the lack of profit maximizing behavior of state firms and supports the contention of the Ljungqvist et al. (2015) study that perverse allocation of capital is stronger when competition is weak.[34] In a detailed study Thomas Rawski (2017) found that despite emerging advantages of state-owned Chinese thermal

---

33. Few group companies are listed, but some subsidiaries of these groups are listed companies.

34. Unlike the steel industry, where entry and expansion of more efficient private firms has steadily eroded the share of output produced by state-owned firms, state firms retain a near monopoly, producing 93 percent of electric power output in 2015 (National Bureau of Statistics of China 2016b, 422, 428). Most of the rest is produced by foreign firms, presumably by industrial firms that generate power for their own use. Prior to the emergence of excess power generation capacity in recent years, these firms commonly installed such capacity to avoid the frequent, widespread disruptions in the domestic power supply.

power generators compared with investor-owned companies in the United States—declining rather than rising costs of constructing new power plants, technological progress allowing Chinese firms to catch up with US firms in terms of thermal efficiency in power generation, and so forth—the cost of generating, transmitting, and delivering electricity in China has risen relative to the United States. The average price electric power users paid in China, which a decade earlier was a third less than in the United States, had converged to the US level by 2014.

Chinese firms in the electric power industry underperform primarily because of overinvestment and excess capacity. In 2003 Chinese thermal power plants operated an average of 5,865 hours per year, very close to the 6,000-hour standard that is considered a high rate of capacity utilization in the global thermal power industry.

Demand for electric power dropped from double digits in 2011 to less than 1 percent by 2015, leading to substantial excess capacity in the industry. But, as Rawski notes, this "did not lead to a major pullback in investment spending as one would expect in a market system."[35] By 2016 the average annual operating hours of thermal plants in China had fallen 30 percent, to only 4,165 hours. In short, absent excess investment, operating hours of existing plants might have been maintained at the previous high level. Profits observed would have been generated with a smaller quantity of assets, leading to lower prices paid by power users and a higher return on assets in the thermal power industry.

Rawski argues that investment continued to surge for at least two reasons. First, an emphasis on scale, a legacy of the planned economy approach of the 1950s, results in "investment projects that establish specific firms or industries as 'key' or 'backbone' elements in their local or sectoral environment may achieve favorable policy treatment." Second, "China's electricity system is dominated by massive state-owned firms whose politically potent leaders, labyrinthine organization, and multiple layers of subsidiaries offer considerable shelter from external scrutiny. These firms' involvement in large numbers of construction projects, no-bid contracts, and related party transactions creates ample opportunities for leaders at all levels to obtain private benefits at the expense of corporate financial outcomes."

The second credible explanation for the increasing underperformance of state firms is the misallocation of capital. The policy of supporting money-

---

35. Rawski's data show, while there was some year-to-year variation, that average annual investment in thermal power generation in 2012 through 2016, when demand was plummeting, was unchanged from the level in 2011.

losing firms with ever larger infusions of bank credit starts at the top. Premier Li Keqiang in a 2015 speech said that China should "avoid having zombie companies," a laudable goal. But the balance of his sentence, "we need to help them, to let them live and live well" provides a rationale for ongoing credit support, regardless of whether their performance improves (McMahon 2018, 36). As shown in the next chapters, government officials, particularly at the local level, are only too happy to ensure the survival of zombies by leaning on local banks to extend more credit. With an assured source of ongoing financial support, these firms have little incentive to improve their performance. Indeed, data from the Ministry of Finance show that by 2016 the losses of unprofitable state firms had doubled as a share of GDP compared with 2005.

Potential for Domestic Convergence

The benign explanations of the underperformance of state firms fall short. The real reasons are that soft budget constraints mean easy credit terms that allow underperforming state companies to continue to expand, complex organizational structures of group companies that appear to offer abundant opportunities for corrupt activities that reduce firm profits, and a large misallocation of capital by Chinese financial institutions. The continued high rate of investment by state electric power generating companies, even in the face of plummeting domestic demand growth, is a good example that captures these problems. But how important are these factors in determining China's growth? How much difference would it make if the performance of laggard state firms converged toward that of private firms? As shown earlier in this chapter, the performance gap is large, but do the lagging state firms control enough assets that convergence would make a significant difference to China's growth?

An international comparative analysis in appendix A shows that China is an extreme outlier in terms of the magnitude of state-owned nonfinancial assets relative to GDP. The extremely high ratio in China is due primarily to the large quantity of assets of state-owned nonfinancial firms and to a lesser extent the value of state-owned land. In 2014 the value of assets of state nonfinancial companies alone was about RMB120 trillion, almost twice the GDP in the same year. Moreover, even as private firms have become the most important source of growth of output, employment, and exports, the assets of state nonfinancial firms by 2016 were RMB155 trillion—almost quadruple the level of 2008, when the global financial crisis erupted (Ministry of Finance 2017b, 366).[36] If one converts this increase into growth in constant prices

---

36. By year-end 2017 these assets had jumped to RMB183.5 trillion more than twice China's GDP (State Council 2018b).

using the official price index for fixed assets, the average annual real growth of assets of state nonfinancial firms was 17 percent, twice the pace of expansion of real GDP in the same period (National Bureau of Statistics of China 2017e, 153).

As shown in figure 2.2, the returns generated by these assets have declined considerably since the global financial crisis and, where reliable direct comparisons can be made, fall far short of the returns generated by assets controlled by private firms.

Two factors account for this rapid expansion in the assets of state-owned enterprises since the onset of the global financial crisis. First, as is well known, in response to the global financial crisis China launched a large-scale, credit-financed stimulus program, which boosted the investment share of GDP from an average of 40 percent in 2006–07 to a peak of 48 percent on average in 2010–11. Although this share has moderated since, it remains above the pre-crisis level (National Bureau of Statistics of China 2017e, 73). A significant portion of this increased investment went to infrastructure projects, including construction of the world's longest high-speed rail network, dozens of additional municipal subway lines, expanded urban water supply and waste water treatment systems, and so forth. State companies control a very large share of the assets created by this investment. This expansion is reflected in the particularly rapid growth of state assets in services (table A.2).

Second, as shown in chapter 4, the share of bank lending flowing to state-owned nonfinancial companies picked up after 2011. This money funded a broad range of state investment projects, many undertaken and financed by so-called local government platform vehicles.

What would have been the effect on China's economic growth if the return on assets controlled by state industrial firms (i.e., manufacturing, mining, utility, and construction companies) rather than falling from the precrisis level shown in figure 2.2 had converged to the level of private industrial companies? In 2015 the return on assets of state industrial and construction companies was only 1.9 percent, while private industrial firms earned 10.6 percent. In the same year the assets of state industrial and construction firms were RMB48 trillion (see table A.2). If these assets had generated the same higher returns as the assets of private companies, value added in industry and construction in 2015 would have been RMB4.2 trillion larger than was achieved.[37]

---

37. Without any data on the returns of private construction companies, this calculation assumes that the returns of private construction companies in 2015 were the same as the returns of private industrial firms, i.e., 10.6 percent.

Similar, if somewhat more uncertain, estimates can be made for the service sector. In the first estimate, in the absence of more recent data, I assume that the 4.9 percentage point gap in the returns on assets of state and private service firms that prevailed in 2008 also prevailed in 2015. Given that state service sector assets in 2015 were RMB91.3 trillion, if the return on assets of state firms had gradually converged to the level of the private sector, service sector value added in 2015 would have been RMB4.5 trillion larger.[38] In the second estimate, I assume that the gap in the returns on assets of state and private service firms widened between 2008 and 2015 by the same roughly 2 percentage points that occurred in the industrial sector. If this estimated gap of 6.9 percentage points in returns had been gradually eliminated, the additional value added generated in the service sector in 2015 would have been RMB6.3 trillion.

Together convergence in both broad sectors would thus imply that real GDP in 2015 would have been at least RMB8.7 trillion, or 12.6 percent larger, and perhaps as much as RMB10.5 trillion, or 15.2 percent larger than actually recorded. To achieve this hypothetical endpoint, real annual growth of GDP between 2007 and 2015 would have to have been 10.2 or 10.6 percent, or as much as 2 percentage points more than the average real growth of 8.6 percent.[39]

---

38. This calculation also assumes that the gap in the return on assets in services shown in table 2.2, which covers 10 components of the service sector, is a good proxy for the difference in returns in the entire service sector. See footnote 19 in this chapter for the four components of the service sector not covered in table 2.2.

39. This is a partial equilibrium analysis that assumes that the growth between 2007 and 2015 of the other components of value-added that make up GDP would not change as a result of higher returns of state companies.

3

China's Failing Strategy to Reform State-Owned Enterprises

The analysis in chapter 2 demonstrates that the faltering economic performance of state firms has dragged down China's growth since the global financial crisis. The Communist Party of China and the government, however, claim to be implementing policies to improve the performance of state companies.

China initiated reform of state companies in the 1980s. The priority the party and government have given to this effort has waxed and waned over the ensuing decades and the results have varied widely—from the relatively successful reforms of the Zhu Rongji era to the near complete failure of the past decade. The current approach has six key dimensions: corporatization of traditional state firms, mergers to reduce the number of state firms, mixed ownership, debt-to-equity swaps, governance reforms, and financial reforms.

Corporatization

The first component of the current reform effort is to accelerate and complete the program of corporatization in which traditional state firms are converted to limited liability companies or joint stock companies. However, corporatization of state firms is not new, rather it has been an ongoing process since the National People's Congress passed the Company Law in 1994, which sets forth the process for converting traditional state-owned companies into corporations. The Company Law created the opportunity for the establishment of limited liability companies and shareholder limited companies (the latter sometimes translated as joint stock companies). Firms with either of these forms of ownership enjoy limited liability, have shareholders and must hold shareholder meetings, maintain shareholder lists, and issue stock certificates to shareholders. In both legal forms of ownership decision making is nominally vested in a board of directors (Zimmerman 2005, 129). The authorities expect these changes in corporate governance to improve efficiency and increase state-owned assets.

By 2011 about 106,000 state-owned companies, about 40 percent of the total number of state-owned companies, had been corporatized; this share rose to 119,000, or 43 percent of all state-owned companies, the following year (National Bureau of Statistics of China 2012, 27–28; 2013, 27–8). At the central level, by the end of 2016 the authorities had corporatized more than 92 percent of the subsidiaries of 101 central state firms.

The gradual and long-term nature of the corporatization process is confirmed in time series data for the corporatization of state-owned industrial firms (table 3.1). There were approximately 120,000 state industrial firms in 1995, the year after the National People's Congress enacted the Company Law (National Bureau of Statistics of China 1999, 421). These were all traditional state firms, known formally as "enterprises owned by the whole people." By 2000 the reported number of these firms had plummeted to only 42,000 (National Bureau of Statistics of China 2001, 401). This decline was not primarily because of corporatization but largely because the reform of state firms undertaken by Premier Zhu Rongji closed or privatized tens of thousands of loss-making state industrial firms. In 2000 there were only 11,000 corporatized state industrial firms, meaning that just under 10 percent of the state industrial firms in existence in 1995 had been corporatized (National Bureau of Statistics of China 2001, 401).[1] By 2006 the number of corporatized state industrial firms was basically unchanged while the number of traditional noncorporatized state industrial companies had fallen to less than 15,000 (National Bureau of Statistics of China 2006, 505). The decline presumably was because some combination of corporatization or exit of traditional state firms, mergers within the universe of traditional state firms, and takeovers of traditional state firms by corporatized state firms more than offset the number of new traditional state industrial firms that may have been created during this period.

The scope of the data reported by the statistical authorities on the number of state industrial firms changed first in 2007 and again in 2011, as indicated in table 3.1. But the share of state companies that were corporatized rose

---

1. The share would have been less than 10 percent if new state corporatized firms had been established between 1995 and 2000.

throughout. By 2015 corporatized state industrial firms controlled more than four-fifths of the assets of all state-owned industrial firms (National Bureau of Statistics of China 2016b, 419, 426).

A new push on corporatization was approved at the Central Economic Work Conference in December 2016 and confirmed by Premier Li Keqiang in March 2017 in his speech to the National People's Congress (Li Keqiang 2017). Shortly thereafter, in July 2017, the State Council formally announced plans to complete the corporatization of all central state firms, except those in the financial and cultural sectors, by the end of 2017 (State Council 2017b). This program will entail corporatizing an additional 3,200 subsidiaries of 69 central state firms.[2]

Further corporatization of state firms, now even more strongly embraced by the government as a policy goal, will not be transformative. As discussed in chapter 2, the financial performance of state-owned enterprises improved dramatically starting in the late 1990s continuing through the middle of the last decade. But it would be hard to credit this improvement to corporatization. As noted above, less than 10 percent of state industrial firms had been corporatized through 2000. The increasing return on assets of state industrial firms starting in the late 1990s and continuing until the eve of the global financial crisis, shown in figure 2.2, appears to be more the result of two factors. First, and most obvious, was exit or privatization of tens of thousands of the worst-performing state firms. Second, the significant increase in competition in the domestic market during China's lengthy negotiations to join the World Trade Organization (WTO) presumably stimulated some state companies to cut costs and adopt new technologies.

It is important to recognize that the increase in competition resulting from lower trade barriers did not begin in late 2001, when China formally entered the WTO. Rather, most of the reduction in tariffs and elimination of nontariff barriers, such as import quotas and import licensing requirements, occurred as part of the negotiation over the terms of China's formal entry. Existing WTO members argued that China had not participated in previous rounds of trade negotiations that had led to significant tariff reductions for existing WTO members and thus China needed to reduce its tariffs as a precondition of entry. During the long, drawn-out entry negotiations, China therefore unilaterally reduced its tariffs from an average statutory rate of 43 percent in 1985, on the eve of its formal request in mid-1986 to join the General Agreement on Tariffs and Trade (the predecessor to the WTO), to 15 percent in 2001,

---

2. Hu Yongqi and Zheng Xin, "Central SOEs reform will be done in 2017," *China Daily*, July 27, 2017, 1.

Table 3.1 Corporatization of state-owned industrial enterprises, 1995–2016 (number of enterprises)

Year	All industrial SOEs		Industrial SOEs with revenues more than RMB5 million		Industrial SOEs with revenues more than RMB20 million	
	Noncorporatized	Corporatized	Noncorporatized	Corporatized	Noncorporatized	Corporatized
1995	118,000	0	n.a.	n.a.	n.a.	n.a.
1996	113,800	0	n.a.	n.a.	n.a.	n.a.
1997	98,600	0	n.a.	n.a.	n.a.	n.a.
1998	64,700	0	n.a.	n.a.	n.a.	n.a.
1999	50,651	49	n.a.	n.a.	n.a.	n.a.
2000	42,426	11,074	n.a.	n.a.	n.a.	n.a.
2001	34,530	12,270	n.a.	n.a.	n.a.	n.a.
2002	29,449	11,651	n.a.	n.a.	n.a.	n.a.
2003	23,228	11,072	n.a.	n.a.	n.a.	n.a.
2004	23,417	12,183	n.a.	n.a.	n.a.	n.a.
2005	16,824	10,676	n.a.	n.a.	n.a.	n.a.
2006	14,555	10,445	n.a.	n.a.	n.a.	n.a.

Year						
2007	n.a.	n.a.	10,074	10,626	n.a.	n.a.
2008	n.a.	n.a.	9,682	11,018	n.a.	n.a.
2009	n.a.	n.a.	9,105	11,395	n.a.	n.a.
2010	n.a.	n.a.	8,726	11,574	n.a.	n.a.
2011	n.a.	n.a.	n.a.	n.a.	6,707	10,393
2012	n.a.	n.a.	n.a.	n.a.	6,770	11,130
2013	n.a.	n.a.	n.a.	n.a.	6,831	11,769
2014	n.a.	n.a.	n.a.	n.a.	3,450	15,350
2015	n.a.	n.a.	n.a.	n.a.	3,234	16,066
2016	n.a.	n.a.	n.a.	n.a.	2,459	16,563

SOEs = state-owned enterprises; n.a. = not available

Sources: National Bureau of Statistics of China (2017e, 413, 420); National Bureau of Statistics of China, data.stats.gov.cn (accessed on September 5, 2017); National Bureau of Statistics of China via Wind Financial Information (accessed on August 1, 2018).

on the eve of its accession (Lardy 2002, 34). In the next 15 years the tariff rate fell by only 5 percentage points to reach 10 percent.[3]

And the significant decline in the number of noncorporatized state industrial firms after 2007 coincided with a sharp decline in the average return on assets of state industrial companies. Perhaps the productivity decline would have been even larger in the absence of the corporatization program, but this would be a tough case to make. In any case, it appears very unlikely that the corporatization of the remaining traditional, noncorporatized state firms, which account for roughly one-fifth of state industrial assets, will transform the performance of state industrial firms.

Mergers

The second key component of China's state enterprise reform strategy is mergers among the largest state companies, invariably orchestrated by the State-Owned Assets Supervision and Administration Commission (SASAC).[4] Formally established in March 2003 at the central government level, SASAC initially was charged with improving the performance of 196 of China's largest nonfinancial state firms, including the three large state-owned oil companies, the three large state-owned telecommunication companies, most of the large state-owned electric power generation and steel companies, the two state-owned electric power distribution companies, the three largest state-owned airlines, and so forth (Lardy 2014, 50).

The economic footprint of the firms under central SASAC far exceeds the impression given by the relatively small number of firms it oversees. But these firms are invariably group companies or holding companies that control multiple subsidiaries. Counting subsidiary firms three levels down from the parent, these group and holding companies in 2010 controlled 23,738 firms, about one-fifth of all state nonfinancial companies. Including 52,371 subsidiaries of

---

3. See data at www.wto.org/english/res_e/statis_e/daily_update_e/tariff_profiles/CN_E.pdf.

4. These mergers typically do not involve any payments, as two state companies are in effect inserted into a newly created third state company. In August 2017, for example, Guodian Group Corporation, one of China's largest power generating companies, and Shenhua Group Limited Liability Company, China's largest coal mining company, merged to form the National Energy Investment Group Limited Company. While the merger creates a firm with more than $250 billion in assets, no value for the transaction was given, presumably since both firms were 100 percent owned by SASAC, as is the newly created firm (Zheng Xin and Lin Wenjie, "Shenhua and Guodian merger gets official nod," *China Daily*, August 29, 2017, 13). Mergers of this type are not included in the data in table 4.1 in chapter 4 or in merger and acquisition activity announced by the China Securities Regulatory Commission.

companies controlled by SASAC entities at the provincial level, SASAC controls three-fifths of all state nonfinancial companies (SASAC 2011, 737). It is little wonder that the US-China Economic and Security Review Commission (2012, 48) characterized SASAC as "the world's largest and most powerful holding company."

Initially, the Ministry of Finance sought to limit SASAC's direct intervention in the day-to-day operations of this universe of large state nonfinancial companies (Naughton 2016a). Rather, SASAC would assume a role like Temasek in Singapore, a financial holding company that manages Singapore's state-owned companies on behalf of the Ministry of Finance (Tidrick 2012). Temasek is charged with generating sustainable returns over a multigenerational period. Actual day-to-day operations of Temasek's portfolio of companies, which includes such iconic firms as Singapore Airlines, are in the hands of professional management. This view, however, did not prevail, and SASAC assumed direct management of its subordinate firms.

Almost immediately after its formation, central SASAC began orchestrating many mergers of firms largely within individual industries; indeed, that appears to have been its major strategy for improving the economic and financial performance of these large state firms.[5] By 2013 these mergers had reduced the number of state firms in the central SASAC universe from around 200 to only 113.

After a brief hiatus between 2012 and 2014, when only five mergers took place, central SASAC resumed its more rapid pace of mergers in the second half of 2015, as shown in table 3.2 (Leutert 2016, 2). The new drive was part of a September 2015 State Council and Central Committee document "Guiding Opinion on Deepening the Reform of State-owned Enterprises" (Chinese Communist Party Central Committee and State Council 2015). By

---

5. In addition to organizing mergers of firms within the same industry, in 2010 SASAC created China Reform Holdings. One of its functions was to serve as a holding company for some SASAC firms in industries where the SASAC universe includes only a single firm. In addition, China Reform Holdings invests both domestically and abroad. It has, for example, taken a 6 percent stake in China Tower, the entity holding the mobile communications infrastructure assets divested by China's three major telecom companies, and it purchased half of the Central Asia Pipeline of PetroChina ("PetroChina: Reform and Substance," *China Daily*, November 27, 2015, 12). Internationally, for example, China Reform Holdings financially backs both Canyon Bridge, a Silicon Valley–based private equity fund that invests in technology assets, and CNIC Corporation, a Hong Kong–registered business that is majority-owned by China's State Administration of Foreign Exchange. See Don Weinland, Leslie Hook, Lucy Hornby, and Peter Wise, "China's Safe agency revealed as holder of 5% stake in EDP," *Financial Times*, June 20, 2018, 15.

Table 3.2 SASAC-orchestrated mergers, 2015–17

Company name	Company name	Date of merger
Shenhua Group	China Guodian Corporation	August 2017
China National Machinery Industry Corporation (Sinomach)	China High-Tech Group	June 2017
China Grain Reserves Corporation (Sinograin)	China National Cotton Reserves Corporation	November 2016
China National Building Materials Group Corporation	China National Materials Corporation (Sinoma)	August 2016
China National Cereals, Oils and Foodstuffs Corporation (COFCO)	Chinatex Corporation	July 2016
China National Travel Service (HK) Group Corporation	China International Trade Services Group Corporation	July 2016
China Merchants Group	Sinotrans & CSC Holding Company	December 2015
China Ocean Shipping Group	China Shipping Group	December 2015
China Metallurgical Group	China Minmetals Corporation	December 2015
China Nam Kwong Group	Zhuhai Zhenrong Corporation	December 2015
CNR Corporation	CSR Corporation	August 2015
China Power Investment Corporation	State Nuclear Power Technology Corporation	June 2015

Source: State-Owned Assets Supervision and Administration Commission of the State Council (SASAC), www.sasac.gov.cn (accessed on September 5, 2017).

the late summer of 2017 this new round of mergers had reduced the number of central SASAC firms to fewer than 100.

But SASAC's own data, reflected in table 3.3, show that these mergers failed to improve the financial performance of the state firms administered by central SASAC; indeed, the opposite is true. Initially, the return on assets of these firms rose slightly to 6.7 percent in 2007 but then plummeted to 3.9 percent in 2008–09 at the height of the global financial crisis. Returns recovered slightly in 2010 but fell to a low of 2.4 percent in 2016 before recovering slightly to 2.6 percent in 2017. But the recovery in 2017 appears to have been driven by a cyclical recovery in global commodity prices, which boosted profits of state companies in some upstream industries, rather than an across-the-board improvement in the operation of SASAC firms. In upstream oil and gas, for example, above-scale companies recorded profits of RMB39 billion in 2017, compared with losses of RMB48 billion in 2016 (National Bureau of Statistics of China 2018c). Since state companies dominate upstream oil and

Table 3.3 Return on assets of central SASAC enterprises, 2005–17

Year	Profits (billions of renminbi)	Assets (billions of renminbi)	Return on assets (percent)	Liabilities/ assets ratio (percent)
2005	641	10,630	6.0	56.1
2006	765	12,192	6.3	55.8
2007	997	14,927	6.7	55.7
2008	696	17,629	3.9	58.4
2009	815	21,058	3.9	60.1
2010	1,143	24,427	4.7	60.8
2011	1,266	28,036	4.5	62.1
2012	1,300	31,357	4.1	62.7
2013	1,300	35,017	3.7	63.4
2014	1,400	38,669	3.6	63.0
2015	1,167	47,581	2.5	66.7
2016	1,233	50,500	2.4	66.7
2017	1,423	54,500	2.6	66.3

Source: State-Owned Assets Supervision and Administration Commission (SASAC), sasac.gov.cn (accessed on March 14, 2018).

gas, this swing in profitability in a single industry accounts for a third of the increased profits of SASAC companies in 2017.[6]

The long-term decline in the return on assets was implicitly acknowledged by the top leaders of SASAC in a 2017 review of SASAC's performance following the 18th Party Congress. They pointed out that between 2012 and 2016 cumulative pretax profits of central SASAC enterprises were RMB6.4 trillion, an increase of 30.6 percent compared with the previous five-year period. But they also acknowledged that assets of these firms by the end of 2016 were 80 percent larger than in 2011, implying but not stating that the return on assets of central SASAC firms had plummeted.[7] SASAC has also publicly acknowl-

---

6. In 2015, for example, state-owned upstream oil and gas firms (i.e., firms in the exploration and extraction end of the industry) accounted for about 85 percent of the revenues and 70 percent of the profits in the industry. Total SASAC profits in 2017 increased by RMB190 billion compared with 2016, so one can estimate that the increase in state oil firm profits (= 0.7 x RMB90 billion) accounted for about a third of the increase in profits of firms in the SASAC universe.

7. "Xiao Yaqing and Huang Danhua attend a news conference on enterprise reform conducted by the State Council Information Office," September 30, 2017, sasac.gov.cn (accessed on October 3, 2017). Xiao and Huang are, respectively, the chairman and vice chairwoman of SASAC.

edged that at the end of 2016 there were 2,041 zombie companies among the subsidiaries of its group companies.[8]

Two additional points are worth underscoring. First, the deteriorating performance of central SASAC firms is particularly telling since this universe of firms is not limited to state industrial companies (for which more complete data are available) but includes many state-owned service sector firms (but not any financial services firms).

Second, SASAC's management has not focused entirely on using mergers to reduce the number of firms under its purview. It has also overseen a stunning increase in the assets of SASAC firms, far beyond what could have been financed with retained earnings. As shown in table 3.3, assets of these firms at the end of 2017 were almost RMB55 trillion, an increase of more than RMB40 trillion over 2005. This increase in assets is fully four times the cumulative after-tax profits generated by these firms over the same period.[9] The increase in the indebtedness of these firms is confirmed in the final column of the table, which shows that the ratio of liabilities to assets for this group of firms rose steadily from about 56 percent prior to the global financial crisis to 66 percent in 2015–17. In short, even though these firms' return on assets, and thus also the retained earnings that could be used to finance investment, was plummeting, they had access to enormous amounts of funding through bank loans and bond and equity issuance. Perhaps the deterioration in the returns of central SASAC firms would have been even more pronounced in the absence of the merger program, but there is no evidence in favor of this hypothesis. The view of the *Financial Times* that the consolidation of Chinese state-owned groups has led to "reduced leverage and higher margins" is complete fiction.[10]

---

8. Zheng Xin, "Exit fund for enterprises can help ease bad debt issue," *China Daily*, July 12, 2018, 14.

9. After-tax profits are calculated by applying the 25 percent corporate tax rate to the annual pretax profit figures in table 3.3. This analysis assumes that depreciation funds, also part of cash flow, are invested to offset real depreciation. The asset figures in the table are net assets, i.e., depreciated assets. Thus, for example, in 2016 net investment was about RMB2.9 trillion, of which only a maximum of RMB1.2 trillion could have been financed with after-tax profits. SASAC firms are required to pay into the state capital management budget, and some listed subsidiaries of SASAC group companies pay dividends to shareholders. Both are financed from after-tax profits, so the amount of investment SASAC firms as a group can finance internally is less than their after-tax profits.

10. Lex, "Sinochem/ChemChina: Trading Places," *Financial Times*, July 3, 2018, 10.

Mixed Ownership

The third key component of the government's plan to transform state companies is mixed ownership—introducing collective or private capital into state firms to rejuvenate them. This program too is not new but, like corporatization and top-down mergers, is a long-standing government policy. Former president Jiang Zemin promoted mixed ownership more than two decades ago. In his speech to the 15th Party Congress in September 1997, Jiang, who served as general secretary of the Chinese Communist Party from 1989 to 2002, argued that public ownership was not limited to state and collective enterprises but included so-called mixed ownership (Jiang Zemin 1997). The Central Committee of the Chinese Communist Party endorsed mixed ownership in a major reform document approved at the 3rd Plenum of the 18th Central Committee in 2013. And the highest level of the government further promoted mixed ownership two years later (State Council 2015b).

By mid-2017 over two-thirds of all central state firms and over half of their subsidiaries had introduced mixed ownership.[11] But the spread of mixed ownership also coincides with a continuous and marked decline in the financial performance of state firms since 2007. It is not clear why the authorities expect that introducing mixed ownership in more state firms will transform them. Some critics of the program argue that mixed ownership is simply a means of bringing in private capital, thereby reducing the burden on state banks to support state companies (Economy 2018, 113).

An example may help to explain the limits of the campaign to promote mixed ownership. In mid-2017 Alibaba and Tencent, two of China's most successful private internet companies, entered into an agreement to set up two research and development centers with China United Network Communications Group Co. Ltd., sometimes referred to as China Unicom Group, China's second largest telecommunications company.[12] Shortly thereafter, Alibaba, Tencent, and two other large private technology firms, Baidu and JD.com, joined a few large state firms to invest RMB78 billion ($11.7 billion) to acquire a 35 percent stake in China United Network Communications Ltd., more commonly known as China Unicom, the Shanghai-listed subsidiary of the group company that holds most of the group company's operating assets. Since retail investors, by definition nonpublic entities, held about

---

11. "Reform of State-Owned Enterprises Has Achieved Great Success Since the 18th Party Congress," July 27, 2017, www.sasac.gov.cn (accessed on July 28, 2017).

12. Ma Si, "Alibaba, Tencent want pieces of telecom giant," *China Daily*, August 2, 2017, 2; Ma Si, "Alibaba to expand in telecom sector," *China Daily*, August 2, 2017, 13.

a third of the shares of this listed company prior to the transaction, it was already a mixed ownership company.[13] The sale of shares to new investors by the unlisted parent, China Unicom Group, reduced its ownership stake in the listed company from 63 to 37 percent.[14]

China's leading technology companies may indirectly benefit from the transaction, since it will provide funds for the cellular carrier to expand its 4G cellular network and develop 5G technology, both of which will further develop the online services these companies offer (Xie 2017).

Whether it will improve the operations of Unicom is less clear. While the transaction was hailed in the Chinese press as a "milestone in SOE reform," little seems to have changed.[15] The four private technology companies have acquired small minority stakes in the Shanghai-listed subsidiary, but as noted above, the subsidiary was already a mixed ownership company prior to this transaction. Digging through the details, it appears as if China Unicom Group and the other large state companies combined retain a 58 percent ownership stake in the listed company, so it remains a state-controlled company (Xie 2017). And China Unicom Group remains 100 percent state-owned and the dominant, controlling shareholder of its Shanghai listed subsidiary. The only innovation of this transaction is that 3 percent of the shares of the subsidiary have been set aside for managers and workers as part of an employee share-holding scheme (Xie 2017).

In 2018 mixed ownership took a negative turn as state companies began to buy up distressed private companies in involuntary transactions. A declining domestic stock market squeezed private entrepreneurs who had pledged their stakes as collateral for bank loans. "Faced with margin calls and cut off from the banking system, some entrepreneurs had little choice but to accept state money."[16]

---

13. The public holds 37.25 percent of the shares of China United Network Communications Ltd., the subsidiary listed in Shanghai, and 25.64 percent of the shares of a second subsidiary, China United Network Communications (Hong Kong) Limited, listed in Hong Kong and commonly known as China Unicom (Hong Kong). These and other details on the ownership structure of the group company and its subsidiaries are available at www.chinaunicom-a.com/wcm/aboutUs/equityStructure (accessed on August 2, 2017).

14. Don Weinland, "Alibaba and Tencent join state-owned groups in $11.7 billion China Unicom Investment," *Financial Times*, August 17, 2017, 12.

15. Fan Feifei, "China Unicom shakeup a milestone in SOE reform," *China Daily*, August 18, 2017, 7.

16. "China Is Buying Distressed Private Companies as Markets Sink," Bloomberg News, October 29, 2018. Available at https://www.bloomberg.com/new/articles (accessed on November 12, 2018).

Debt-to-Equity Swaps

The fourth component of the government's program to reform state-owned enterprises is debt-to-equity swaps in which banks forgive loans outstanding to an enterprise in exchange for equity in the firm.[17] The logic is straightforward—the profitability of a firm that is only marginally profitable or even loss making will be improved if more of its funding takes the form of equity rather than debt. Premier Zhu Rongji used this approach as part of the state enterprise restructuring program he implemented beginning in the late 1990s and the government resurrected it in a modified form starting in 2016 (State Council 2016b).

In practice, to date debt-to-equity swaps have been limited in scale, partly by design and partly because of difficulties in implementation. By the end of 2017 banks had reached swap agreements with only 102 companies with a total amount of RMB1.6 trillion. However, only RMB230 billion in swaps had been executed, a rounding error relative to RMB132 trillion in loans outstanding to nonfinancial corporations at the end of 2017.[18] Almost all swaps have been with state-owned rather than private companies.[19] To encourage more swaps the central bank in mid-2018 cut the required reserve ratio of almost 20 banks by 0.5 percentage point, freeing up about RMB500 billion, on the condition that the banks use the funds to complete debt-to-equity projects already approved but not yet executed.[20]

The central bank guidelines on the swap program suggest its limits. First, zombie firms are not eligible to participate in the program. The swaps are aimed primarily at firms with "special mention loans" outstanding, one step

---

17. Banks do not directly own equity. They inject capital into a legally separate, wholly owned vehicle, which purchases the loans from the bank and then swaps them for equity in the initial borrower. The banks thus technically avoid violating the Commercial Bank Law, which prohibits them from directly owning equity in nonfinancial corporations. Banks, however, remain at risk because if the vehicle can't eventually sell the equity for at least the amount of the initial loan, the value of the vehicle will fall, an event that would have to be reflected on the bank's consolidated balance sheet.

18. "Five Large Banks Have Signed Debt-to-Equity Swaps Valued at RMB1.6 trillion," *Securities News*, June 12, 2018, www.xinhuanet.com/money (accessed on June 25, 2018).

19. According to public information on 81 cases of debt-to-equity swaps reached through September 2017, involving a total of RMB1.3 trillion, only one case involved a private company; the rest were all state companies, mostly controlled by local governments. UBS Global Research, "SOE reform and bank NPL series (1): Debt-to equity swaps—positive but likely modest impact," October 10, 2017.

20. China International Capital Corporation, "PBoC announces another relatively broad-based RRR cut of 50bp," Macroeconomy Research, PBoC Watch, June 24, 2018.

above nonperforming in China's loan classification scheme,[21] or normal loans. Second, in principle pricing of swaps should be market-oriented. But very few firms are publicly listed, which would provide at least a starting point for negotiation on price. So in practice the book value of the firm frequently is the starting point, followed by lengthy negotiation on the size of the discount to be applied to the book value. Third, to encourage mixed ownership, outside nonfinancial investors should match the banks' funding. Finally, the nonfinancial investors should participate in the management of the firm after the swap. Negotiation on the nature of this participation could be a major hurdle. An outside nonfinancial investor presumably would seek control, probably a deal breaker for incumbent managers.

Governance Reforms

A few years ago, when the government launched an initiative to divide state nonfinancial firms into two categories—commercial and public service—China seemed to be moving in the direction of requiring most state enterprises to focus primarily on improving their financial performance (Naughton 2018, 380–81; Song 2018, 362). Clearly most state enterprises would be classified as commercial and judged primarily based on profitability and other familiar financial metrics.[22] Loss-making firms in this universe thus would no longer have ongoing access to bank loans and other sources of finance, presumably meaning that continued loss making by these firms would lead to bankruptcy or a takeover by another firm. On the other hand, a small share of state firms that provide public services, such as local utility and subway companies, which operate in a regulated price environment, can't easily be judged solely on profitability and other financial metrics. These firms may lose money because the state sets prices at a low level, so they were to be judged partly on the quality of the goods and services they provide. Commercial state firms were also authorized to raise money from outside investors, even to the point where the state's share fell under 50 percent, thus tying in with the mixed ownership reforms.

---

21. China has a five-tier loan classification system: performing, no overdue payments; special mention, payments overdue less than 90 days; substandard, payments overdue more than 90 but less than 180 days; doubtful, payments overdue more than 180 but less than 360 days; and loss, payments more than 360 days overdue. The last three categories comprise the universe of nonperforming loans.

22. Some commercial enterprises in sectors key to national security would be judged in part on additional, unspecified criteria.

SASAC, which was responsible for dividing the firms it controls into the two categories, reportedly completed the process in 2014. But, for unexplained reasons, this mapping of firms was rejected, and the process restarted. SASAC again declared the process complete in 2017 both at the central level and at all 31 provincial-level SASACs, but no information has been released on the number of firms in each category or which firms they are (Naughton 2018, 380–81). The most plausible conjecture for this result is that powerful vested interests at large state companies that were tentatively classified as commercial were able to fend off the attempt to make their firms responsible for their own profits and losses.

Financial Reforms

The first essential step in financial reform is for the regulatory and other authorities to obtain more accurate information on the banks themselves. Chinese financial authorities understand that the reported levels of nonperforming loans to state-owned enterprises are understated, resulting in an overstatement of bank profits. After all, since 2011, the China Banking Regulatory Commission[23] has allowed banks to classify loans in the "overdue but not impaired" category in their long-form financial statements, which more than 200 banks have done to dodge categorizing bad loans as nonperforming (Bedford 2018). Thus, profits are overstated by uncertain amounts, making evaluation of banks on financial metrics problematic. That, in turn, makes it possible for banks to continue to lend to loss-making companies.

In the first half of 2018 the China Banking and Insurance Regulatory Commission took two steps that should lead to more accurate measurement of the quality of loans in the Chinese banking system. First, in early 2018 the regulator reduced the amount of funds banks have to set aside to cover bad loans in order to reward banks that more accurately report nonperforming loans.[24] For example, required provisions as a share of nonperforming loans would be reduced from 150 to 120 percent, conditional on fulfilling certain other conditions.[25] A few months later the regulator, in a further attempt to

---

23. The China Banking Regulatory Commission (CBRC) and China Insurance Regulatory Commission (CIRC) merged to form China Banking and Insurance Regulatory Commission in April 2018.

24. Jiang Xueqing and Chen Jia, "Bad debt disposal seen improving," *China Daily*, March 18, 2018, 15.

25. The required level of provisioning for the five categories of loans (see footnote 21) are 1 percent; 2–3 percent; 25–30 percent; 50–60 percent; and 100 percent (Bedford 2018, 12). Provisions are also required to reach 150 percent of total nonperforming loans.

improve bad loan recognition, eliminated the practice of classifying loans as "overdue but not impaired." City and rural commercial banks, which are most disproportionately affected by the new rule, are allowed to delay implementation until 2019 (Bedford 2018).

There is no visible progress on the second critical reform in the financial sector—the capture of second-tier banks by local officials. Even when these banks are listed, local governments often exercise control. The more general problem is that there is "no substantial competition between fully private and publicly owned banks" (IMF 2018). The number of truly private domestic banks is tiny and their role in the financial sector is quite limited. Similarly, foreign banks are so few that they do not enhance competition in the financial sector. Central bank governor Zhou Xiaochuan long sought to further open the financial system to more foreign competition. He argued that too much protection for domestic institutions weakens the industry and can lead to financial instability.[26] Zhou appears to have been the architect of the financial liberalization program finally announced in late 2017.[27] The program entails lifting caps on foreign ownership, which have long prevailed in banking, asset management, securities, and insurance.[28] Once fully implemented, this program could contribute to more efficient allocation of financial resources, especially bank credit. However, foreign banks are likely to play a small role in the dozens of smaller administrative regions where city and rural commercial banks operate, so local zombie companies may continue to get bank support.

Conclusion

It is not surprising that corporatization, mergers, mixed ownership, debt-to-equity swaps, and governance and financial reforms have thus far failed to improve the performance of state-owned companies. The first three programs appear to involve more form than substance. Most of the state firms that are corporatized and adopt mixed ownership remain state-controlled, meaning that the state continues to be the majority or at least the dominant, controlling shareholder. And the group companies that have been merged to date

---

26. Bloomberg News, "Zhou's Jibe at 'Lazy' Banks Signals China More Open for Business," June 19, 2017, www.bloomberg.com (accessed on March 6, 2018).

27. Bloomberg News, "China PBOC to Draft Package for Financial Market Opening, Sources Say," September 18, 2017, www.bloomberg.com (accessed on September 20, 2017).

28. "China's financial groups opened to foreign owners," *Financial Times*, November 13, 2017, 8.

under SASAC guidance remain 100 percent state-owned.[29] The Organization Department of the Chinese Communist Party in many cases continues to appoint the top management; the Party Committee within each firm retains a central role in major corporate decisions; and there is little or no increase in transparency.

While the State Council (2017a) advises strengthening the role of the board of directors in state companies converting to corporate ownership, these boards appear to be largely window dressing. In market economies, the key function of any corporate board is to select and remove top management, decisions that are only nominally controlled by the board in Chinese state companies. Technically the Organization Department nominates and boards confirm candidates to the top three management positions in large state companies. But there are no known cases where the board of a state-controlled company has failed to confirm the nominees chosen by the party's Organization Department.

Since they are subject to stricter disclosure requirements, transparency is improved in corporatized state-owned firms that are subsequently listed on the Shanghai or Shenzhen stock exchanges. But it is important to keep in mind that this group of firms is a tiny subset of corporatized state firms in China. For example, of the almost 120,000 corporatized state-owned nonfinancial firms in 2012, only 966 were listed on either the Shanghai or Shenzhen Stock Exchange.[30]

SASAC's merger program has not improved corporate governance but has reduced competition and created new monopolies, impeding innovation, productivity, and financial performance of SASAC firms.

While the objectives of the debt-to-equity program are laudable, its scale to date has been too small to reduce the leverage or improve the financial performance of China's state-owned companies.

Finally, the corporate governance and financial reform programs have barely gotten off the ground, making the goal of judging state banks or state firms based on financial metrics elusive.

---

29. In mid-2018 SASAC announced that it would begin introducing mixed ownership in group companies.

30. Data from Wind Financial Information.

4

The Path Back to Market-Oriented Economic Reform

To sustain China's economic growth at the moderately high levels of recent years, or perhaps pushing those rates even higher, Chinese leaders must set new priorities. The path forward should entail a combination of policies that would reduce the role of the party and government in the economy and return China to a path of market-oriented reform. China should compel those running state-owned companies to raise the return on their assets, which might require transferring underperforming assets to more productive private firms. The Chinese also need to allocate bank loans and bond and equity issuance more efficiently and reduce political interference in the management of enterprises.

An essential way to achieve these aims would be to increase competition within each economic sector. To do that, the state should reduce barriers to entry by private firms, which are high in many service industries such as telecommunications, financial intermediation, education, and health as well as in upstream oil and gas. These steps would increase competitive pressure on underperforming state companies. For example, in the oil and gas industry, three state-owned oil giants—the China National Petroleum Corporation, China Petroleum and Chemical Corporation (Sinopec), and the China National Offshore Oil Corporation—have maintained near total dominance. The reason is that the Ministry of Land and Resources historically has allocated potential oil and gas blocks only to these companies. Only in 2015 were tenders opened to private companies, although in the first auction of six blocks, only one went to a private company. A second auction open to private investors was scheduled for 2017 but at the time of writing it was not clear whether the auction took place.[1]

To reduce the assets of state companies that continue to operate at a loss in the face of greater competition and that cannot or will not improve their management, the government should step in to facilitate more market-driven mergers and acquisitions. The goal would be to let more efficient firms acquire some or all of the assets of troubled state firms. In addition, the state should compel persistently unprofitable state companies—many of them so-called zombie firms—to declare bankruptcy and exit the economy altogether. Bankruptcy typically means that creditors seize the assets of the bankrupt firm and auction or sell them to other firms. Thus, the liquidation of these bankrupt firms would provide another opportunity, in addition to merger and acquisition activity, for more productive firms to acquire underperforming state assets. The government should promote additional reforms in the financial sector, encouraging banks and capital markets to allocate capital more efficiently to healthier economic sectors and companies. Instead, the current environment allows massive quantities of funds to flow to prop up ailing state-owned companies rather than requiring them to shut down if they can't achieve greater efficiency.

For a variety of reasons, China's reform program falls short in several dimensions. This chapter lays out measures to help China return to a path of market-oriented reform.

Reduce Barriers to Entry

As already noted, the return on assets of state service firms is lower than the returns of their industrial counterparts, and a large share of the financial losses of state firms is generated in the service sector. One potential cause is the relatively high entry barriers in services compared with those in manufacturing. In many service sectors, restrictive licensing hinders entry for both foreign and private domestic firms. One indicator is the relatively high share of investment in services undertaken by state versus private firms. Manufacturing has long been very open to domestic private firms, as reflected in the investment shares of private and state firms (see chapter 2). By 2014, state-owned firms accounted for only 8 percent of investment in manufacturing, while domestic private firms accounted for 77 percent.[2] On the other hand, the share of investment in services undertaken by state firms in the same year was 42

---

1. Zuo Shuo, "Auction of oil, gas sites to boost energy exploration in Xinjiang," *China Daily*, December 15–17, 2017, 19.

2. Collective and foreign firms undertook the balance of the investment.

percent—five times their share in manufacturing. Private firms accounted for 37 percent of investment in services, only half the share they had attained in manufacturing (National Bureau of Statistics of China 2015, 324–25).

The OECD Services Trade Restrictiveness Index shows that China also has high restrictions on trade in services. This index reflects a combination of factors, including barriers to entry by foreign firms, barriers to competition (i.e., restrictions on entry by domestic firms), lack of regulatory transparency, and other discriminatory measures. Across 14 different services, China is almost as open as the OECD average in only three—architecture, engineering, and computers. In most of the 11 other services, for example banking, insurance, telecommunications, and logistics, China is two to four times more restrictive than the OECD average (IMF 2016c, 42).

In addition, the government has long maintained oligopolistic market positions of the China National Petroleum Corporation (CNPC), the China Petrochemical Corporation (Sinopec), and the China National Offshore Oil Corporation (CNOOC), which collectively controlled 85 percent of the income from the extraction of oil and natural gas in 2015 (National Bureau of Statistics of China 2016b, 422, 428). The returns of the first two firms are very low, in part because they are fully integrated, controlling both upstream and downstream activities. For example, for decades both firms have had in-house oilfield service units.[3] In contrast, most of the rest of the major multinational oil firms have long contracted out oilfield services to specialized companies such as Halliburton, Schlumberger, or dozens of less well-known firms. The absence of competition in this and other critical specialized functions in the oil exploration and production process in China drives up costs and reduces profits of China's oil majors.[4]

Promote Mergers and Acquisitions and Bankruptcy

China has very little market-oriented merger and acquisition (M&A) activity, i.e., bottom-up activity initiated by individual firms bidding to take over underperforming assets controlled by other firms. Only a few private firms have

---

3. In contrast, CNOOC, by far the most efficient of the three Chinese oil majors, merged its various oilfield service units and in 2002 listed the new company as China Oilfield Services Ltd. (Bloomberg, "CNPC mulls small-cap oilfield services listing," *China Daily*, September 14, 2016, 13).

4. In 2016 CNPC contemplated injecting its various oilfield units into Daqing Huake Co., a small-cap listed company owned 55 percent by two CNPC subsidiaries. That approach was rejected and in late 2017 CNPC began to restructure its fragmented oilfield service units in preparation for an initial public offering.

Table 4.1 Domestic merger and acquisition activity, 2007, 2015, and 2016

Year	Number of transactions	Value (billions of renminbi)
Announced		
2007	1,745	541
2015	5,963	2,524
2016	4,593	2,190
Completed		
2007	1,076	318
2015	2,336	1,435
2016	2,543	1,422

Source: Wind Financial Information (accessed on August 17, 2017).

acquired assets from underperforming state companies. Rather, most M&A activity appears to be top-down, state-orchestrated mergers among the universe of large state firms (see chapter 3).

Table 4.1 shows annual data on domestic M&A activity in China since 2007.[5] There are several key takeaways. First, both the number and value of transactions, whether measured on an announced or completed basis, have grown rapidly. For example, the value of completed transactions more than quadrupled by 2016 compared with 2007. Second, despite this rapid growth, the value of M&A activity remains very modest, relative to both the market capitalization of the universe of listed companies and the size of the Chinese economy. Annual announced transaction volume in the peak years of 2015–16 averaged only RMB2,360 billion ($370 billion). Completed transactions were about 40 percent less, averaging 2 percent of GDP. In contrast in 2015–16, the total completed deal flow within the United States averaged $1.7 trillion, roughly 10 percent of US GDP.[6] Third, based on the number of announced transactions in 2014–15, the average transaction value in China is tiny, about

---

5. Bloomberg is another source of data on Chinese M&A activity. However, compared with the data from Wind Financial Information shown in table 4.1, the Bloomberg series appears to include only transactions involving listed companies.

6. Data on M&A activity cited for both the United States and China exclude the value of cross-border transactions. US data are from www.statista.com, a publicly available source, and are quite close to data available from Dealogic, available by subscription.

RMB450 million, or roughly $70 million, whereas in the United States individual transactions of $10 billion or more are not unusual.[7]

China especially needs more transactions in which private firms assume control of some or all the assets of underperforming state companies. One positive example is the restructuring of Dongbei Special Steel Group Co., a 100 percent state-owned company based in Dalian, Liaoning province (in northeast China), which in 2016 defaulted on RMB7 billion in bonds held by more than 100 creditors. Shen Wenrong, a private entrepreneur who made his fortune in the steel industry, invested RMB4.5 billion and assumed a controlling 43 percent ownership of Dongbei.[8] The previous state equity was entirely wiped out, though the Liaoning provincial government gained a 10 percent stake by injecting RMB1 billion as part of the restructuring. Small creditors that owed less than RMB500,000 were repaid in full and other creditors had to choose between repayment of 22 cents on the dollar or exchanging their debt for equity. This latter group of creditors ended up owning 47 percent of the restructured company.

Bankruptcy is relatively rare in China and does not appear to contribute significantly to putting assets into the hands of more efficient firms. According to the Supreme People's Court of China, in 2016 China's legal system accepted only 5,665 enterprise bankruptcy cases, of which 3,602 were adjudicated, including 525 reorganizations (Supreme People's Court 2017). China had 14.6 million firms in 2015, so the roughly 3,000 exiting firms accounted for a minuscule share (National Bureau of Statistics of China 2016b, 22).[9] In 2014 about 28,000 and 24,000 enterprise bankruptcy cases were filed in

---

7. One reason that the value of the average M&A transaction is so small in China is that some transactions involve purchases by one company of a small minority stake in another company. For example, in 2017 Changjiang Electricity bought a 4.69 percent stake in Guotou Electricity. Both firms remained separately listed, state-controlled companies after the transaction. Data are from Wind Financial Information.

8. Shen Wenrong is the chairman of Shagang Group, the largest private steel company in China, with four production facilities in Jiangsu and Henan provinces. See Gabriel Wildau and Xinning Liu, "China steel magnate rescues 'zombie' enterprise," *Financial Times*, November 2, 2017, 14.

9. Some of the bankruptcy cases in recent years have been of group companies, and typically creditors who bring these cases include some of the subsidiary firms of the group in the bankruptcy filing. Thus, the number of firms involved in bankruptcies is presumably somewhat larger than the numbers cited in the text, which are based on cases, not number of firms. For example, the 2016 bankruptcy of the Dongbei Special Steel Group Co. included two of its subsidiaries. See "Dongbei Special Steel formally enters bankruptcy restructuring," Xinhua, October 10, 2016, reuters.com (accessed on August 2, 2017).

the United States and Germany, respectively, compared with about 3,700 in China (IMF 2016a, 20). Relative to the size of their economies, the United States and Germany had, respectively, 4.6 times and 17.5 times the number of bankruptcy cases as China.

Prior to 2007 bankruptcy was infrequent because of insecure creditor rights. The 1986 Bankruptcy Law as well as the Civil Procedure Law and the Security Law, which took effect in 1991 and 1995, respectively, all provided substantial legal protection for creditors. In practice banks in the mid-1990s that filed against debtor firms frequently recovered only a very small share of the loans outstanding. The main reason is that administrative rules overrode the laws and required that proceeds from the liquidation of bankrupt firms be applied first to unpaid wages and taxes, as well as unmet pension and social insurance contributions. Banks got repaid only if there were funds left over. In this circumstance, banks rarely initiated proceedings against creditors (Lardy 1998, 141). The revised 2007 Bankruptcy Law reiterates that secured claims, such as bank loans, have priority over unpaid wages, taxes, and social insurance contributions. Courts, however, retain enormous discretion in bankruptcy cases; perhaps they are continuing to give priority to employees over banks.

Reform the Financial Sector

Historically China's state-owned banks lent almost exclusively to state firms. These mostly unprofitable firms accumulated nonperforming loans so large that China's banking system became insolvent by the mid-1990s (Lardy 1998, 119). Subsequently the government orchestrated a massive recapitalization of the largest state-owned banks, attracted significant equity investments in these banks by foreign financial institutions, and ultimately listed them on domestic and international markets. In the process, the government increased the pressure on large state banks to operate on a commercial basis and assume responsibility for their own profits and losses, a requirement initially set forth in the 1995 Commercial Bank Law.

The government also sought to increase competition by licensing new shareholding banks and city commercial banks. As a result the share of financial system assets controlled by the largest state-owned banks gradually declined from 70 percent in 1986 to 60 percent in 1995 and only 25 percent by the end of 2016 (Lardy 1998, 80; IMF 2017d, 60).[10]

---

10. These figures understate the shrinking role of the largest state banks since the beginning of 2007, when the Bank of Communications was added to the group of state-owned commercial banks. Since 2010 this group of five banks has been referred to as "large commercial banks."

Figure 4.1 Flow of loans to nonfinancial enterprises by ownership, 2010–16

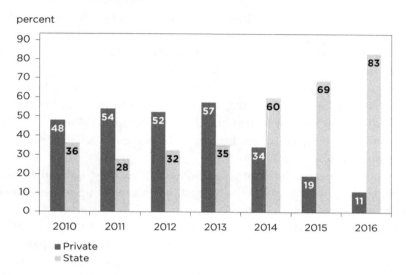

percent

Private
State

Note: The data include renminbi loans made by Chinese banks, urban credit cooperatives, agricultural credit cooperatives, and foreign banks and exclude loans made by finance companies, trust companies, auto finance companies, and village and township banks (China Banking Society 2011, 322).
Source: China Banking Society (2011, 322; 2012, 369; 2013, 367–68; 2014, 341–42; 2015, 326–27; 2016, 357–58; 2018, 313–14).

These developments in the financial sector, combined with further opening up to private firms in manufacturing and services, increased the share of corporate loans flowing to private firms, which were now driving China's economic growth. These firms were more efficient, generating much higher profits relative to their assets, which made them on average more creditworthy than state companies. By 2011 domestic-currency loans by banks and other financial institutions to privately controlled nonfinancial enterprises accounted for 54 percent of all new corporate loans, well ahead of the 28 percent share flowing to state companies (Lardy 2014, 105).[11]

But, as shown in figure 4.1, since 2011 the share of domestic-currency corporate loans to state firms, including local government financing vehicles, has surged. By 2016 the state share had jumped 55 percentage points to 83 percent, while the share of new corporate loans to private companies had

---

11. The private firm share of the stock of loans outstanding in the same year was only 36 percent, demonstrating clearly that the share of new lending to private firms in earlier years must have been much smaller than 54 percent.

fallen 43 percentage points to only 11 percent.[12] New loans to private corporations in 2016 were only RMB630 billion, a decline of 75 percent from the 2011 peak of more than RMB2.5 trillion (China Banking Society 2018, 313–14).[13]

It appears that private companies were able to partially offset their declining access to loans from financial institutions by stepping up their borrowing from nonbank financial institutions, i.e., shadow banks. Starting in 2016, however, the authorities began to restrict the operations of the less well-regulated shadow banking system in order to reduce financial risk. As a result, private firms were squeezed out, leading to the first ever decline in their share of investment (see figure 1.1).

While the central bank compiles and publishes these data on financial system lending by ownership with a significant lag, more up-to-date data on lending by microfinance companies support the view that private firms continued to be squeezed out after 2016. Microfinance companies, which lend overwhelmingly to individuals and small private firms, grew rapidly after 2008, when formal guidelines on microfinance companies were first issued by the People's Bank of China and the China Securities Regulatory Commission (Lardy 2014, 114). But, as shown in figure 4.2, this rapid growth came to an abrupt halt after 2014. The volume of outstanding loans leveled off at just under RMB1 trillion.

Another important indicator of crowding out of investment by private firms in industry is the large amount of working capital they hold in comparison to state firms. Working capital is simply current assets minus current liabilities.[14] The main component of the former is receivables, i.e., money due from customers, while the main component of the latter is payables, i.e., money due to suppliers. State industrial firms are so successful at delaying payments to their suppliers that, as a group, they have negative working capital—their current liabilities exceed their current assets. Note that since payables

---

12. The increase between 2011 and 2016 in the share of new corporate loans flowing to state companies is 12 percentage points greater than the decline in the share of new corporate loans flowing to private companies because the share of new corporate loans flowing to collective firms, foreign firms, and firms from Hong Kong, Macau, and Taiwan also fell.

13. Part of the increase in the share of loans to state companies may be due to the reclassification of some public institutions as enterprises (Lardy 2014, 139) and of some local government financing vehicles, previously treated as agencies, as enterprises. This reclassification does not, however, explain the sharp drop in the amount of absolute lending going to private firms.

14. A current asset is expected to be converted to cash within a year. A current liability must be paid within a year.

Figure 4.2 Loans outstanding by microfinance companies, 2010–17

billions of renminbi

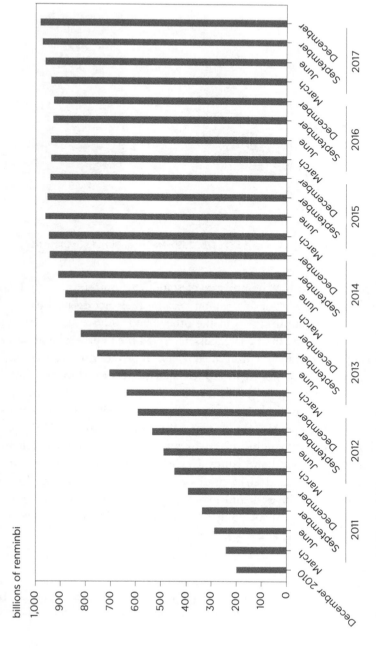

Source: People's Bank of China quarterly data via Wind Financial Information.

Figure 4.3 Profits and investment of state-owned enterprises, 2011 and 2015

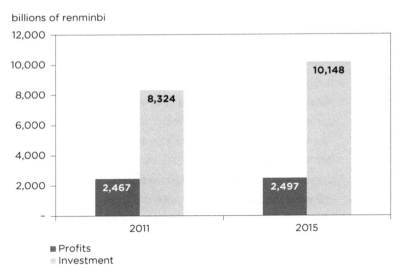

billions of renminbi

- Profits
- Investment

Sources: Ministry of Finance (2017b, 369); National Bureau of Statistics of China, data.stats.gov.cn; author's calculations.

and receivables within the universe of state firms cancel out, state firms as a group have negative working capital because their net delayed payments are primarily to private firms.[15] On the other hand, private firms have positive working capital, i.e., their current assets exceed their current liabilities. Again, payables and receivables within the universe of private firms cancel out. So, in effect, private companies are forced to make indirect loans to state companies, meaning that the magnitude of investment by private firms is below what one would expect based on their return on assets and their ability to borrow from banks, while the inverse is true for state firms (Gatley 2015, 2018).

The rapidly expanding claim of state companies on bank loans and funding through bond and equity issuance is clearly demonstrated in figure 4.3. Between 2011 and 2015 profits of state firms increased by less than 2 percent while their investment expanded by more than 20 percent. The difference was increasingly made up by funds from the state budget and larger bank loans, bond issuance, and stock offerings.

---

15. Some of the delayed payments of state companies could be to foreign firms operating in China. These firms account for about one-quarter of output in China's industrial sector but a much smaller share in services. Thus, the bulk of the payables of state firms is likely delayed payments to private firms.

Lending to private firms by China's formal financial system has declined in recent years for three possible reasons, other than crowding out and the undermining of private property rights. First, private internet, e-commerce, and technology firms such as Alibaba, Baidu, Tencent, and Xiaomi are booming and achieving stratospheric market capitalizations. But the assets of these and other technology firms are primarily intangibles such as software and design, rather than plant and equipment. Thus, they are generally capital light. Moreover, these and other technology firms have relied primarily on venture capital and private equity in their early stages and, more recently, public offshore listings. Alibaba, for example, was funded from the outset in the late 1990s by private equity funding from Softbank, Goldman Sachs, Fidelity, and other offshore institutional investors. In 2014 Alibaba's initial public offering on the New York Stock Exchange, the largest ever, raised $25 billion. In 2017, 88 Chinese technology companies raised $7.6 billion in global public offerings, and markets expect even larger offshore fundraising by private technology companies in 2018.[16] The success of Alibaba and many other private Chinese technology firms has not depended, and likely will not depend, on access to loans from Chinese banks.

However, there are problems with the argument that the rise of new economy, capital-light firms that rely primarily on private equity and initial public offerings for funding is a major reason for the decline in the share of lending by Chinese financial institutions to private companies. First, in 2015 there were 10.6 million private companies in China producing about three-quarters of China's GDP (National Bureau of Statistics of China 2016b, 22).[17] The handful of listed internet and high-tech companies, although wildly successful based on their market valuations, account for a minuscule proportion of private firms and likely a very small share of China's GDP.[18] Second, while private firms have been able to raise increasing funds through private equity, venture capital, and angel investor firms, these funding sources remain relatively small compared with the magnitude of bank loans previously extended to private firms. In 2017, for example, aggregate corporate financing by domestic private equity, venture capital, and angel investors was RMB551 bil-

---

16. Louise Lucas and Emma Dunkley, "Chinese tech IPOs set to eclipse last year's total as Baidu unit eyes $2.7 bn listing," *Financial Times*, March 20, 2018, 18.

17. Private firms produced an estimated 70 percent of GDP in 2013 (Lardy 2014, 94). Given that private firms substantially outperformed state firms in industrial value-added growth in both 2014 and 2015, private firms likely produced three-quarters of GDP by 2015.

18. In addition to Alibaba, listed Chinese internet companies include Tencent, listed on the main board of the Hong Kong Stock Exchange in 2004, and Baidu, listed in New York in 2005.

lion.[19] While most of this financing appears to have supported private firms, it remains tiny compared with total new lending by domestic financial institutions plus bond issuance of local governments, which was RMB19.44 trillion in 2017. Moreover, most of this private equity, venture capital, and angel funding appears to be directed toward startups in an important but relatively narrow space—internet, artificial intelligence, and so forth—rather than the broader universe of private firms. The venture capital and private equity subsidiaries of internet giants Alibaba, Tencent, and Baidu have become major sources of finance for high-tech startups.[20]

A second possible reason for the decline in lending to private firms by China's formal financial system is the rising importance of fintech firms, which provide an alternative source of finance to private firms. Ant Financial, for example, provides credit lines to more than a million entrepreneurs and shop owners selling on Alibaba's Taobao e-commerce platform (Hau et al. 2017). The extension of credit, surprisingly, is automated, based on data generated by billions of transactions on the Taobao platform, and continuous monitoring of transactions allows the firm to extend credit to less creditworthy borrowers.

While Ant Financial has extended credit to hundreds of thousands of firms, many with low credit scores, the firm's lending does not materially offset the decline in lending to private businesses through the formal financial system. First, a large share of the firm's borrowers had no previous access to traditional bank credit. So only a small share of Ant Financial's loans could be substituting for credit previously extended by the formal financial system. Second, the size of the average loan extended by Ant Financial from September 2014 through July 2016 was only RMB20,000, presumably a boon to a small, credit-starved entrepreneur selling on Taobao but too small to be transformative for a larger private firm. Third, while the total outstanding credit from Ant Financial has grown rapidly, in February 2016 it was only RMB86.7 billion, an amount that

---

19. Data are from Wind Financial Information. Private equity and venture capital funds in China manage much larger funds, more than RMB7 trillion, according to research firm Zero2IPO. But this number includes funds that have already been invested and funds that have not been deployed. See David Blair, "Growing future money trees," *China Daily*, April 14–16, 2017, 4.

20. Henny Sender, "Funds for AI start-up fan concerns over Chinese tech bubble," *Financial Times*, January 23, 2018, 20.

is barely large enough to be a rounding error in the RMB142.5 trillion in loans outstanding from the formal financial system at the same time.[21]

A third potential explanation of the decline in the flow of bank loans to private firms is that an increasing number of private firms have gained access to the domestic equity market, offsetting the decline in bank lending to these firms. Initial public offerings by private firms, for example, rose from 239 in 2011 to 377 in 2017, but initial public offerings by state firms were only 31 in 2017. While the proceeds from the average state firm's initial listing far exceed those of private firms, the relatively large number of private firm listings in 2017 meant that these firms accounted for three-quarters of fundraising through initial public offerings, seemingly supporting this third explanation. State firms, however, dominate secondary offerings, which accounted for four-fifths of the RMB1.1 trillion raised on the domestic equity markets in 2017. Taking all these factors into account, the share of total equity fundraising flowing to state firms increased from 35 percent in 2011 to 44 percent in 2017, reinforcing the rising share of bank lending flowing to state firms.[22]

In short, the argument that the decline after 2013 in the share of lending by banks and other financial institutions to private firms reflects the rise of capital-light, new economy firms or the rise of fintech or the expanding equity financing of private firms and thus has little or no implication for China's future growth is not well founded. Yes, private firms in the technology space appear to be generously funded by domestic and foreign venture capital and private equity firms, but these firms are a very small slice of the private firm universe. The rise of fintech may eventually disrupt China's financial system, but it is now too small to be a significant source of finance for private companies. Similarly, evidence does not support the idea that increased equity funding of the broader universe of private firms has offset their declining access to bank loans.

Indeed, by 2018 official voices raised concerns about the undermining of private property rights and the crowding out of private investment. President Xi Jinping in late September publicly emphasized the importance of private firms to the success of the Chinese economy. The following month Liu He chaired a meeting of China's top financial regulatory body that endorsed specific measures for easing financial difficulties of private firms.[23] Early the fol-

21. People's Bank of China, "Report on Financial Statistical Data February 2016," March 11, 2016, www.pbc.gov (accessed on March 11, 2016).

22. Author's calculation based on data from Wind Financial Information.

23. Chen Jia, "Policies expected to ease financing pressure," *China Daily*, October 22, 2018, 1.

Figure 4.4   Leverage ratio of state industrial companies, 1998–2016

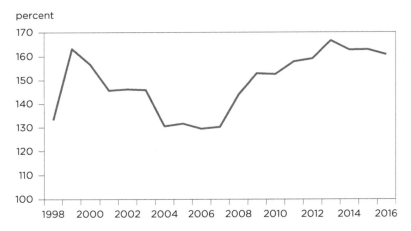

Sources: National Bureau of Statistics of China, data.stats.gov.cn (accessed on March 14, 2018); National Bureau of Statistics of China via Wind Financial Information (accessed on August 1, 2018).

lowing month central bank governor Yi Gang announced a series of new policies to increase bank loans and bond and equity financing for private firms. A few days later Guo Shuqing, the head of China's bank and insurance regulator, put forth a specific target that no less than 50 percent of new corporate loans should go to private companies over the next three years.[24] Of course, it remains to be seen whether these initiatives will alleviate the crowding out of private investment.

Figure 4.4 sheds light on whether state companies have productively used the increased funding from bank loans and other sources of finance external to the firm. It shows that the leverage ratio (the ratio of liabilities to equity) of state industrial firms fell in response to the enterprise reforms initiated by Premier Zhu Rongji in the late 1990s but has risen considerably since 2007 and by 2015 was back to the previous peak level of 1999. As explained in chapter 2, a rising average leverage ratio for state firms is inevitable when these firms borrow to expand, but two-fifths or more of them are loss making, meaning they are unable to fully amortize their loans. Over time, to continue to invest, firms with this wedge between the cost of capital and return on assets will have to borrow increasing amounts to pay the interest on their existing liabilities, thus increasing the leverage ratio (Liu 2016, 100).

---

24. Zhu Liangtao and Denise Jia, "Top Bank Regulator Calls for More Lending to Private Sector," November 9, 2018, www.caixinglobal.com (accessed on November 9, 2018).

The sharp increase since 2013 in the share of bank lending flowing to state companies, even as these borrowers' leverage ratio was rising, their average return on assets persistently falling, and their interest coverage ratio consistently shrinking, is nothing short of astounding. It calls into question the assessment that Chinese banks "have become profitable, stable and well-managed institutions...that comply with most international standards of financial management...have reasonably effective corporate governance...,[and] look not much different from modern banks in other major economies" (Stent 2017, 37).

As noted in the introduction, Chinese firms that consistently lose money, borrow additional funds to pay interest on prior outstanding debt, and have a persistently rising leverage ratio are referred to in official documents, academic studies, and press reports as "zombie companies."[25] The State Council defines zombies as companies that suffer three consecutive years of losses. Other studies have used different criteria. One study, for example, classified firms with two successive years of earnings before interest and tax (EBIT) less than interest due at market interest rates as zombies. Such companies stay in business not only because of subsidies via an expanding flow of credit but also because sometimes the state awards them overpriced projects (Tan, Huang, and Woo 2016).

Even prior to the global financial crisis, zombie firms were a significant feature of China's economic landscape. Tan, Huang, and Woo (2016, 38) analyzed detailed firm-level data on China's industrial sector in 2005–07 and found that around 15 percent of all industrial firms should be classified as zombies and that state-owned enterprises had the highest proportion of zombies. They estimated that the exit of zombie firms and the reallocation of their labor and capital to more efficient firms would lift annual industrial growth by more than 2 percent, employment growth by almost 1 percent, and total factor productivity growth by 1 percent (Tan, Huang, and Woo 2016, 53).

The International Monetary Fund (IMF) has provided updated estimates of zombie industrial firms based on a similar definition but more recent firm-level data (Lam et al. 2017). On its baseline definition of zombie firms, the study found that 6.5 percent of industrial firms were zombies in 2016 and that these firms accounted for 16.2 percent of the debt of all industrial firms. State-owned enterprises, which accounted for only 17 percent of the profits of in-

---

25. Zombie firms are not unique to China. The term was widely used to describe firms in Japan that were kept afloat by bank loans, dragging down the country's growth in the 1990s. Zombie firms have also been seen as contributing to the slowdown in productivity growth in OECD countries since the late 1990s (Andrews, McGowan, and Millot 2017).

dustrial firms, accounted for 55 percent of the debt of zombie industrial firms (National Bureau of Statistics of China 2017f). Extrapolating the analysis to the entire universe of firms, the IMF study found that zombie firms accounted for 9 percent of China's corporate debt in 2016.

For three reasons, the IMF study likely understates the current share of zombie firms and the magnitude of their debt. First, unlike the industrial surveys used in the Tan, Huang, and Wu study, which included all industrial firms with more than RMB5 million in sales, the IMF study had to look at firms with more than RMB20 million in sales.[26] There is a strong negative correlation between firm size and return on assets, i.e., smaller firms on average have much lower returns. The IMF study, which excludes all small firms, probably underestimates the share of zombie firms.

Second, given the decline by two-thirds in the average return on assets of state industrial companies between the pre–global financial crisis period analyzed by Tan, Huang, and Woo and the 2016 data presented in the IMF study, it is surprising that the IMF estimate of the share of zombie industrial companies in 2016 (6.5 percent) was less than half that in the earlier period (15 percent in 2005–07). Although the output share of state industrial firms declined over this period, one would have anticipated that, given the almost 4 percentage point drop in the average returns of these state firms, the share of the still large number of industrial state-owned firms falling into the zombie category would have increased.

Third, given that a large share of the losses of state firms is generated by firms in the service sector (see chapter 2), one would expect that the share of the total debt of all nonfinancial corporations accounted for by all zombie firms would be substantially higher than the share of debt of industrial firms accounted for by zombie industrial firms. Instead, the IMF study finds that the share of debt of all zombie firms (9 percent) is just a bit over half of the (16.2 percent) share of the debt of zombie industrial firms.

The expanded claim of state companies on China's financial resources reflects the high priority the party and the government have placed on sustaining rapid growth in most of the past decade. Two factors strongly suggest that increased lending by local financial institutions to local zombie state companies accounts for a large share of the increase in credit outstanding to the nonfinancial corporate sector. First, local state enterprises persistently un-

---

26. In 2011, the National Bureau of Statistics of China increased the threshold for inclusion in the industrial survey to RMB20 million in sales. To enable better comparison of the annual surveys over time, the IMF deleted firms with sales below RMB20 million in the surveys before 2011.

derperform compared with firms controlled by the central government. For example, the reported return on assets of local state firms in both 2015 and 2016 was only 1.3 percent compared with 2.5 and 2.2 percent for central firms in the two years, respectively (Ministry of Finance 2016b, 2017a). The extremely low average return on assets of local state firms means that the share of these firms that persistently lose money is likely higher than the share of centrally controlled state firms that were loss making in the same years. In short, loss makers among state firms appear to be firms controlled at the local level. When measured by assets local state firms on average were only three-fifths the size of centrally controlled state firms but they are so much more numerous that at the end of 2016 they accounted for over half of the assets of all state enterprises (Ministry of Finance 2017b, 366).

Second, much of the credit growth after the global financial crisis has come through expanded lending of city and rural commercial banks, predominantly owned and controlled by local governments, rather than through the expanded lending of the four or five largest state-owned banks that are controlled by Central Huijin, a unit of China Investment Corporation, China's sovereign wealth fund. The share of banking and financial system liabilities of city and rural commercial banks expanded from 7.5 percent in 2007 on the eve of the global financial crisis to 21 percent by the end of 2016.[27]

Promotions of local party and government officials depend heavily on economic growth and employment, particularly the avoidance of "social instability," which might occur if local zombie companies are scaled back or closed. The concern of local officials has two dimensions. First, and most obvious, they want to avoid layoffs. Second, they want to avoid losing fiscal revenues they can use to support local public services and investment. Even firms with negative operating profits must pay the value-added or business tax, both tied to sales rather than profits. Revenues from the business tax, now phased out, were retained by local governments; only a small share accrued to the central government. Historically, one-quarter of the revenue from the value-added tax (VAT), paid by industrial firms, also was retained locally. And, as the government began to expand VAT to cover services, these revenues were entirely retained locally. Since mid-2016, when VAT covered all services on a nationwide basis, VAT revenues, from both industrial and service firms, have been shared equally between the central and local governments. To avoid losing these sources of tax revenue, local officials frequently pressure local financial institutions to continue to support money-losing local state companies

---

27. Data are from Wind Financial Information.

(McMahon 2018, 37), which in turn have to continue to pay these taxes. The marked increase in the share of lending by banks owned and controlled by local governments suggests this phenomenon is widespread.

Financial sector reform has at least two key components. First, bank accounting standards, particularly the criteria for classifying nonperforming loans, must be strengthened so that the financial metrics reported by banks are more meaningful. It will continue to be difficult for the bank regulators to crack down on banks extending more loans to loss-making state firms if the result of these loans is not reflected in accurate data on the magnitude of nonperforming bank loans. Second, the authority of the bank regulator must be strengthened so it can end the capture of smaller banks, particularly city and rural commercial banks, by local officials. Chinese data on nonperforming loans are weak, allowing banks to report inflated profits. When nonperforming loans are underreported, loan loss provisions (funds set aside to cover potential losses on loans) are less than Chinese banking regulations call for, artificially boosting reported bank profits. In its most recent Financial System Stability Assessment on China, the IMF notes that "certain small and medium-sized banks have large amounts of loans that are 90 days past due (DPD) but are not classified as non-performing" (IMF2017d, 45). Officially China has adopted the Basel Committee's guidelines requiring all loans that are 90 days past due to be classified as nonperforming. But it has introduced a loophole allowing banks to classify overdue bank loans with sufficient collateral or guarantees by third parties as "special mention" or even performing. In addition, since 2011 banks have been allowed to report corporate loans overdue more than 90 but less than 180 days, previously always treated as nonperforming, as "overdue but not impaired" (Bedford 2018, 2). These practices reduce the funds that banks must set aside as provisions, artificially propping up banks' reported profits and disguising the growth of loans to loss-making firms.

Second, the Fund notes that "local governments have important ownership stakes in lower tier banks and—in many cases—exercise control." Local officials, in effect, have captured city and rural commercial banks and some other lower-tier financial institutions and have forced them to extend loans to underperforming local companies. The "overdue but not impaired" loans of these institutions would push up the ratio of nonperforming loans of city and rural commercial banks by a third, from 1.5 to 2.0 percent. In contrast, the five largest state-owned banks, which are not subject to local capture, have no "overdue but not impaired" loans, so their reported average ratio of nonperforming loans of 1.6 percent appears to be more accurate (Bedford 2018).

Improve Governance

Governance of state-owned enterprises should more clearly focus on financial performance metrics, such as return on assets. To the extent that state-owned firms are assigned social objectives, these should be clearly defined with costs covered by transparent subsidies provided through the state budget. Such a system would enable managers and owners of state firms to focus on financial performance indicators. The current governance arrangement appears to assign a higher priority to maintaining employment than maximizing profits, allowing zombie firms to operate seemingly indefinitely while generating returns far below the social cost of capital. This arrangement must be replaced with one in which loss-making (net of budget subsidies covering social objectives) enterprises exit through bankruptcy or merger.

Some argue that when a country with many preexisting distortions embarks on economic reform, it should provide transitory protection, including subsidies, to firms rather than opting for big bang reform in which all prices are quickly liberalized and firms are immediately subject to hard budget constraints (Lin and Shen 2018, 132). China has been through four decades of reform and can hardly be considered a transition economy. China's ongoing subsidies to almost half of all state enterprises cannot be rationalized by arguing that China is still a transition economy.

5

Prospects for Further Economic Reform

Many see China's recent economic slowdown as reflecting the natural slowing of what is now a more mature, upper-middle-income country rather than an emerging market. Carl Minzner (2018, 61), for example, believes that the rapid growth of exports and investment that powered growth for more than three decades is tapped out and we should now expect a China characterized by permanently lower growth. Some compare China with Japan. It had a multi-decade run as the world's fastest growing economy. But following the bursting of its credit-fueled asset price bubble in the early 1990s, Japan suffered a decade of extremely modest growth. China too has had a massive increase in credit since the global financial crisis. Might it be embarking on a path similar to that of Japan?

This study rejects both the natural slowing argument and the analogy with Japan. Comparing China with Japan is correct on one level—policy matters. Japan's slowdown was not inevitable; it was induced by policy (Posen 1998). Fiscal policy in Japan in the 1990s was notably weak, a major error given in-sufficient aggregate demand, and the Japanese government long delayed the needed cleanup of the banking system, slowing the growth of credit to the real economy. The natural slowing argument fails to consider that appropri-ate economic reforms have the potential to sustain China's growth around 8 percent, perhaps slightly more. As noted earlier, achieving this potential also depends on a favorable global environment. Policy stasis, on the other hand, could slow growth. On another level the comparison of China today with Japan in the 1990s is also somewhat misleading. As noted in chapter

2, Japan's sustained rapid growth resulted in substantial convergence of per capita income toward the US level. Thus, by the 1990s, convergence was no longer pushing up Japan's potential growth (Posen 1998, 17). In contrast, China's per capita GDP today is at a very low level compared with the United States, so convergence potentially could continue to sustain or even slightly push up China's growth.

This book argues that burgeoning trade surpluses in the years prior to the global financial crisis pushed China's growth above potential. About half of the slowdown in China's growth in 2009–16 compared with 2005–08 was the result of the necessary moderation of its trade surplus, compounded by the weak recovery of global trade. Much, if not most, of the rest of the slowdown reflects the weakening performance of state-owned firms.

This study further argues that China's growth is no longer benefiting from a shift in the locus of investment from underperforming state firms to more productive private firms. Indeed, the increasing access of state firms to financing from banks and capital markets is raising the share of investment undertaken by China's least efficient firms, pushing China's growth further below its underlying potential as well as increasing financial risk.

Two counteracting forces appear to be determining China's current pace of economic growth. On the positive side, a rebalancing of the sources of economic growth, with services and private consumption assuming increasing roles as the growth of exports and investment wanes, is holding up China's economic growth. For example, growth would have slowed even more since the global financial crisis if consumption as a share of GDP had continued to decline after 2010 rather than steadily rising. This rebalancing seems likely to persist since it is caused by a combination of secular trends and government policies that are unlikely to be reversed.

On the negative side, the deteriorating profitability of state firms and the financial sector's increasing misallocation of resources are holding China's growth to a pace below potential and simultaneously increasing financial risk. In terms of ownership, private firms continue to generate high returns and only a few are unable to fully cover their cost of capital. But insecure private property rights and crowding out mean that the growth of private relative to state investment moderated considerably after 2011 and appears to have slowed further in both 2016 and 2017.[1] State firms, on the other hand, have gained

---

1. In 2017 total fixed asset investment rose 7.2 percent while state investment was up 10.1 percent (National Bureau of Statistics of China 2018a). At the time of writing data on fixed asset investment for private and privately controlled firms in 2017 had not been released. But nongovernmental (*minjian*) investment was up only 6.0 percent. Nongovernmental, sometimes

greater access to funding from banks and capital markets in recent years. These firms have thus increased their share of investment, even when their returns are declining both in absolute terms and relative to average returns of private firms. Moreover, more than two-fifths of state firms persistently lose money, i.e., they can't fully cover their cost of capital. This appears to explain both the sharp rise in the leverage ratio of state industrial firms since the global financial crisis and the observation that monetary policy is becoming less effective in supporting China's growth (Chen and Ratnovski 2018). The reasons why extension of more credit since the global financial crisis has been accompanied by slower rather than more rapid growth are simple. First, since 2011, a growing share of new credit has been flowing to state-owned companies that are generating lower returns. Second, part of this increased flow of credit is not supporting new economic activity at all but rather reflects the capitalization of interest on previous loans that zombie companies can't pay.

The various benign explanations of the deterioration of the financial performance of state-owned firms are far from convincing (see chapter 2). State firms do not appear to enjoy a systematically declining cost of capital that would make their falling average returns since the global financial crisis consistent with profit-maximizing behavior. The concentration of state firms in more capital-intensive industries, which are more cyclical in an economic slowdown, also does not appear to be a major contributor to the decline in the financial performance of state firms. Excessive social obligations of state firms once did penalize these firms in financial terms relative to private firms, but these burdens have been largely eliminated over the past two decades.

What are the political and economic impediments to implementing a more far-reaching economic reform program that would both improve the efficiency of state-owned firms and allow more productive private firms to gain control of the assets of firms that continue to underperform?

---

mistranslated by Chinese statistical authorities as private, is a classification that includes not only private firms but also collective firms, cooperative firms, collective joint enterprise firms, and other joint enterprise firms. The actual controlling ownership of this latter group of firms is usually unclear, so in this study, except in this footnote, I have eschewed relying on data based on the nongovernmental classification. However, private firms dominate the nongovernmental category, so the conclusion is that, as in 2016, state investment in 2017 grew more rapidly than private investment.

Obstacles to Reform of State-Owned Enterprises

The fundamental obstacle to implementing far-reaching economic reforms in China is the top leadership's view that, while state-owned firms may be a drag on China's economic growth, they are essential to maintaining the position and control of the Chinese Communist Party and achieving the party's strategic objectives (Economy 2018, 15–16). These strategic objectives are outlined in the Made in China 2025 program and other industrial policies and include achieving domestic dominance and global leadership in a range of advanced technologies. Other strategic objectives are international, notably the Belt and Road Initiative, where state-owned construction companies such as the China State Construction Engineering Corporation Limited are major contractors for building roads, rail lines, power plants, ports, and other infrastructure in countries participating in the initiative. The top ten construction and engineering companies active outside China, all state-owned, are almost four times more leveraged than the top ten global non-Chinese construction and engineering companies.[2] State firms that serve the interests of the party do not lack financial support.

China's leadership also hopes that state firms will grow to become so-called national champions and compete with multinationals based elsewhere. In remarks on a panel at the Boao Forum in 2018, Xiao Yaqing, head of the State-Owned Assets Supervision and Administration Commission (SASAC), emphasized that SASAC firms were becoming larger and ever more capable of serving a global role. He touted the RMB26 trillion in top-line revenue of central SASAC firms in 2017 but failed to mention that the profitability of these firms had declined precipitously since the global financial crisis. China's leadership seems to have willingly accepted reduced profitability, slower growth, and the greater financial risk associated with high leverage to be able to exercise more economic and political control (Naughton 2018, 377–78).

A second obstacle to far-reaching economic reform is the Chinese leadership's fear of social instability. Reform will inevitably downsize the state sector and cut millions of jobs. It almost certainly would also slow growth in the short run. Private firms will not be able to immediately expand to offset the loss of employment and output of state firms, and they will not seek to take over state firms that they judge would remain unprofitable even with better management and reduced interference from the state. Slowing growth, even in the short run, would exacerbate many of China's current economic challenges.

---

2. James Kynge, "China's Belt and Road project drives debt fears," *Financial Times*, August 8, 2018, 3.

Even in the absence of major reform, however, social unrest has been growing, with labor protests almost doubling between 2014 and 2016, a period when aggregate employment in state firms was stable. Apparently in response, Premier Li Keqiang in 2016 said that, while excess labor needs to be reduced, workers can't be laid off—they must be transferred to new jobs. Similarly, Xiao Yaqing, the head of SASAC, in 2016 said that "protecting the interest of employees of state-owned enterprises will be a major task." And official media have stated clearly that layoffs of the type and scale that occurred during the reform of state companies in the 1990s will not occur (Economy 2018, 109).

From the perspective of external observers, the leadership's fear that reducing employment at underperforming state companies will lead to social instability is difficult to understand for several reasons. First, by 2016 employment in state-owned companies stood at 46 million, a seemingly huge number. But these employees represent only 11 percent of urban employment. The comparable numbers in 1999 were 59.8 million and 27 percent (National Bureau of Statistics of China and Ministry of Human Resources and Social Security 2018, 7–8, 262–63; Lardy 2014, 139).[3] Downsizing of employment in state firms today could be less challenging than two decades ago because of the dramatic increase in the share of urban employment in private firms and a commensurate decline in the share of employment in state firms.

Second, even a far more systematic reform effort than has been evident in more than a decade will not necessitate eliminating most jobs in state firms. When competition increased in response to reforms and opening up in the late 1990s and early 2000s, a large share of state-owned industrial enterprises improved their operations, raised their profitability, and thus remained in production. There is no reason to not expect a similar response to another far-reaching reform program. Not all state firms are inevitably slugs.

Third, as noted in chapter 2, 37 million jobs, mostly in state firms, were lost as a result of the reforms initiated in the late 1990s. There is little evidence that this downsizing and the accompanying moderation in economic growth led to massive labor unrest.[4] Laid-off older workers were eligible for severance

---

3. China does not disaggregate data on employment in state enterprises into its urban and rural components. The percent figures cited are calculated based on the assumption that all employment in state enterprises is in urban areas. The magnitude of employment in state-owned firms in 1997, when layoffs were already underway, was larger than in 1999, the baseline used in the text, but data on state employment for 1997 or 1998 are not available.

4. Economic growth averaged 10 percent in 1995–97 but slowed to an average of 8.1 percent in 1998–2001. Estimating how much if any of this economic slowdown was the result of shrinking state-owned enterprises is beyond the scope of this book.

pay, which helped many of them tide over until they were eligible for pensions. Younger workers received extended unemployment benefits and access to various retraining programs. Many found new jobs in the rapidly growing private sector. Despite the layoff of 27 million workers from underperforming, mostly state-owned firms, between 1998 and 2004, urban employment in this period expanded by 65 million, a little over 30 percent (National Bureau of Statistics of China and Ministry of Human Resources and Social Security 2018, 7–8).

Fourth, employment in state companies today is very different from 20 years earlier. As analyzed in chapter 2, housing, medical, social, and retirement benefits of workers in state firms are no longer tightly tied to employment status. And lifetime employment in state companies, already eroding somewhat since the 1990s (Lardy 2014, 19–20), is mostly a thing of the past. Workers who have found jobs in state firms since the mid-1990s mostly work on term contracts. Under the provisions of the Labor Contract Law, which took effect in January 2008, workers can gain a so-called open-ended contract only after 10 or more years of consecutive employment under fixed-term contracts or the completion of two consecutive fixed-term contracts (National People's Congress 2007). And many of these contract workers are hired by so-called labor dispatching units, independent firms that provide contract workers to enterprises. While these contracts must be for a minimum of two years, in intervals when the contracting firm can't provide work, these dispatched contract workers receive only the local minimum wage, typically less than 20 percent of the average regional wage. These changes presumably should make the loss of employment in a state company a less traumatic financial and economic experience than 20 years ago and thus be less likely to lead to labor unrest.

According to conventional wisdom in both China and the West, President Xi Jinping is China's strongest, most secure leader since Deng Xiaoping or perhaps even since Mao Zedong. His fear of labor unrest suggests conventional wisdom is wrong.

A third obstacle preventing China's leadership from pursuing far-reaching economic reforms is the fear of financial instability, which, of course, in turn could lead to social instability. Since late 2016 the leadership has recognized the need to slow growth of credit to reduce the financial risks associated with the massive buildup of domestic debt since the global financial crisis. Deleveraging has made some progress, particularly in reducing the complex layers of credit involving nonbank financial institutions. This progress is reflected most clearly in the decline in borrowing by nonbank financial institutions in the interbank market, the major source of funding of these institutions.[5]

But reducing the liabilities of heavily indebted state-owned companies is challenging because the most heavily indebted firms are likely the ones that have borrowed to finance ongoing losses over the last decade. Since their operating profits are insufficient to fully service their existing debts, deleveraging will be very slow and in some cases impossible. An aggressive reform program could lead to widespread loan defaults, putting extreme pressure on city commercial banks and other locally owned financial institutions that have lent large sums to local state-owned firms.

China's leadership thus seems to prefer to proceed slowly, hoping that the cyclical recovery in the profitability of state-owned enterprises, which began in 2016 and picked up further in 2017, particularly in upstream industrial firms that benefited from the global recovery in some commodity prices, will continue and that the need for substantial additional fundraising to bolster the capital of weak financial institutions can be avoided.

A fourth obstacle to far-reaching reform is the opposition of vested interests, including the top management of large SOEs, some government bureaucrats, and many local political officials. The capacity of entrenched government bureaucrats to undermine central reform programs is well known and understood, even in economies that are more market-oriented than China. The power of the bureaucracy in Japan in the post–World War II period, at least up to the administration of Prime Minister Junichiro Koizumi, is well documented. And in China the increasing reliance of President Xi on a growing number of so-called small leading groups, all under the party and almost all chaired by the president, to shape and oversee the implementation of policy, is widely believed to be an end run around vested interests in the government and elsewhere that don't fully share his policy priorities (Minzner 2018, 29, 105–106).

The problem of vested interests at the local level is particularly acute in China. Local political leaders are keenly aware that local protests and unrest can derail promotions and even end careers prematurely. Moreover, China has long had a system of incentives for local bureaucrats to encourage growth. The system rewards local leaders who meet established targets for GDP growth

---

5. Bank claims on nonbank financial institutions expanded at an average annual pace of more than 50 percent from 2012 through the first half of 2016. Growth then plummeted into negative territory, i.e., claims shrank, almost continuously through April 2018 (Wind Financial Information).

and expanding fiscal revenues with cash rewards and increased chance of promotion (Naughton 2017, 10). Given that local state enterprises are much less profitable than state enterprises controlled by central SASAC and central ministries, it is not surprising that these local leaders have little enthusiasm for reform programs that might reduce local employment and local fiscal revenues. These leaders appear to have substantial capability to coerce local banks to prop up underperforming local firms.

This problem is hardly new—it was much in evidence in the 1990s (Pei 1998, 327–28). Party secretaries and government leaders at the provincial or municipal level inevitably outranked heads of state financial institutions in their jurisdictions. These latter officials often were unable to reject requests for additional loans to money-losing state companies. Over time this lending led to a massive accumulation of nonperforming loans and the insolvency of China's largest banks (Lardy 1998, 119).

One of the key provisions of the reform and recapitalization of the Chinese banking system in the late 1990s was a regulation requiring local bank officials to seek approval from their superordinate administrative level for loans. Thus, for example, when a provincial governor or party secretary demanded that the head of a provincial branch of the Industrial and Commercial Bank of China (ICBC) extend additional credit to a provincially owned enterprise, the head of the branch in theory should have been able so say, "I am sorry, I am not authorized to approve such a loan, but I would be happy to relay the application to our head office in Beijing." Since the president of ICBC would outrank a provincial governor or party secretary, the loan officer at the head office in principle could review the loan application based primarily on its commercial merits rather than on political considerations, confident that if the head office turned down the loan there would be no major political repercussions. If a city mayor requested that the city branch of ICBC make a loan to a municipally owned firm, a similar process was to apply, i.e., the loan would be referred to the ICBC branch in the provincial capital, where the head would inevitably outrank the local official who requested the loan.

The central bank also abolished its provincial-level branches and replaced them with nine regional, supraprovincial branches headed by more senior officials who would outrank provincial administrators and party officials. The goal was to further insulate local state banks from political interference in their lending decisions. According to Premier Zhu Rongji, "the power of provincial governors and mayors to command local bank presidents is abolished as of 1998" (Lardy 2003, 198).

It is not clear how well this system worked in practice, undoubtedly imperfectly. But over time an array of smaller regional banks, notably city commercial banks, displaced the dominant role of the largest 4 or 5 state-owned banks, thus undermining the system. These smaller banks are also state-owned, but the owners are mostly municipal governments and their geographic scope of operation is frequently limited. Thus, when a mayor directs the local city commercial bank to extend additional credit to a money-losing enterprise owned by the municipality, the head of the bank can't refuse—there usually is no head office to hide behind.

While one can't prove causation, the growing share of loans extended by banks owned primarily by local governments appears to reflect the rapid growth of lending to state enterprises controlled by these subnational governments.

Reasons to Be Optimistic

The four impediments to a more aggressive economic reform program are real. But other factors pushing in the opposite direction may eventually dominate, putting China back on the path of more market-driven reform.

First, and perhaps most important, "no issue is as central to the Chinese leadership's legitimacy as ensuring rising income levels" (Economy 2018, 95). Slowing economic growth ultimately undermines achieving this goal, particularly when one considers the additional fiscal resources the government needs to clean up the environment, improve the safety of food and medicines, further build out the social safety net, and meet other needs that are central to realizing President Xi's Chinese Dream—the rejuvenation of the great Chinese nation.

Second, the current extremely gradualist approach to reform appears to be inconsistent with the goal of deleveraging and reducing financial risk. Under the current reform program, leverage of state-owned companies is falling at a glacial pace. In 2017 the average ratio of liabilities to assets of central SASAC firms fell by a minuscule 0.4 percentage point—from 66.7 percent in 2016 to 66.3 percent (table 3.3 in chapter 3). At that pace it will take well over two decades to reduce this ratio to the less risky level that prevailed prior to the global financial crisis.

And the headwinds against achieving even this slow pace of deleveraging are growing. The US Federal Reserve began to raise interest rates starting in late 2015, a process that is likely to continue for some time. In response the Chinese authorities also began to nudge domestic interest rates higher, presumably to head off or at least mitigate capital outflow pressures. This headwind is increasing for two reasons. First, interest rates in the developed world are likely to rise further. The European Central Bank in mid-2018 announced that it would suspend its monthly bond purchases (so-called quantitative easing) by the end of the year and likely would begin to raise interest rates in the latter part of 2019. The Bank of England has also signaled its intention to exit from its quantitative easing program, which eventually will lead to rising interest rates in the United Kingdom. Thus, pressure on China's authorities to raise rates seems certain to increase. Higher domestic interest rates in China, however, will increase the burden of debt repayment, making it less likely that even the current modest pace of deleveraging can be sustained.

Second, the fear that bilateral trade frictions with the United States that began in 2018 will slow China's growth has prompted Chinese authorities to slightly increase liquidity and lower short-term interest rates in the second half of 2018, inevitably leading to somewhat faster credit growth, slowing and perhaps even temporarily reversing progress on deleveraging. Thus, China's leadership may opt for a more aggressive financial overhaul that would entail a wholesale write-off of the loans of heavily indebted state companies and a hardening of budget constraints on these companies, as well as a capital injection for China's smaller financial institutions where nonperforming loans appear to be concentrated.

Third, ultimately China's pursuit of state-driven growth is inconsistent with the repeated pledges of President Xi to further open China's economy and promote globalization. In his Davos speech in January 2017 President Xi gave a robust defense of globalization, arguing that "economic globalization has powered global growth and facilitated movement of goods and capital, advances in science, technology and civilization, and interactions among peoples." And he pledged that China is "committed to a fundamental policy of opening-up," and "will expand market access for foreign investors" and "strengthen protection of property rights."[6] President Xi subsequently elaborated on these themes, notably in his speech at the Boao Forum in April 2018.

Yet many observers outside China are skeptical about these speeches. The greatly enhanced role of the state in resource allocation in recent years, including detailed industrial policies issued by China's State Council, contrasts sharply with the party's claim in 2013 that the market would decide the allocation of resources. The ongoing subsidies to large numbers of money-losing state companies put foreign firms at a disadvantage, in selling not only in China's domestic market but also in international markets. China's state-driven and frequently state-financed acquisition of foreign high-technology companies feeds the fear in the West that China seeks to dominate technologies of the future, leaving the United States and other Western economies to dominate traditional, lower value-added, slower-growing industries. Thus, the

---

6. "Jointly Shoulder Responsibility of Our Times, Promote Global Growth," January 17, 2017, www.china.org.cn (accessed on May 25, 2018).

United States, the United Kingdom, and the European Union are implementing tougher reviews of both inbound Chinese direct investment and exports to China by Western multinationals, to stanch the flows of advanced technologies to China.

President Xi thus has multiple incentives to implement the market-oriented reform strategy outlined at the Third Plenum. First, it provides the best prospect over the medium term of boosting China's annual growth by a percentage point or slightly more, dovetailing with the party's high-priority goal of ensuring rising personal income for China's citizens and providing additional fiscal resources to alleviate environmental degradation, improve food and drug safety, and build out the social safety net.

Second, resuming market-oriented economic reforms, including eliminating subsidies to state companies and modifying industrial policies so they treat both domestic and foreign firms equally, is essential for China's further integration into the global economy and for legitimizing President Xi's claim that China will provide leadership for a more globalized economy. Without such reforms, major trading partners are likely to restrict China's access to their markets and limit its ability to acquire advanced technology through acquisitions of their firms. China cannot credibly advocate for further globalization, which depends on free and open markets, when its domestic policies continue to move in the opposite direction.

Appendices

Appendix A
Assets in China

There are several sources of information on the value of assets in the Chinese economy. The Ministry of Finance compiles and publishes the most detailed balance sheet data on state nonfinancial enterprises. Its website has monthly data starting in 2007 on the assets, liabilities, equity, profits, revenue, and other economic indicators for state and state-controlled nonfinancial enterprises.[1] The ministry's periodic reports provide monthly and year-to-date information. In addition, the ministry's annual yearbook provides more disaggregated annual data for the same variables (Ministry of Finance 2016a, 2017b). For example, the yearbook disaggregates total state enterprise assets, liabilities, and so forth in three dimensions: by level of government, i.e., central government and local governments; by province; and by various components of assets and liabilities. Moreover, the annual yearbook data include information on government, social, and other organizations and thus are somewhat broader in scope than the monthly reports.[2]

---

1. The ministry's monthly reports are available at http://qys.mof.gov.cn/zhengwuxinxi/qiyyunxingdongtai/. The reports cover 94 state enterprises owned by central departments, 113 state enterprises supervised by SASAC, five state enterprises supervised by the Ministry of Finance, and local state enterprises. See www.mof.gov.cn/previewqiyesi/zhengwuxinxi/gong-zuodongtai/201407 /t20140728_1118640.html.

2. The assets in this category have grown very rapidly from 6 percent of the total in 2009 to 16 percent in 2015. This expansion is because of the government's program to corporatize certain public institutions not previously classified as enterprises. These are now referred to as "public institutions managed as enterprises" (企业化管理事业单位).

Other government agencies also release information on national assets, including those of private as well as state firms. These include the National Bureau of Statistics, which began systematic research on compiling a national balance sheet in the 1990s. Its annual statistical yearbook has long provided data on assets of industrial firms, disaggregated both by ownership (state, private, and foreign) and by subsector, as well as data on assets of some service sector firms, again disaggregated by ownership. The bureau also publishes the *China Statistical Yearbook of the Tertiary Industry*, which provides some information on assets in the service sector (National Bureau of Statistics of China 2014). The annual yearbook of the State-Owned Assets Supervision and Administration Commission (SASAC 2011) provides data on both nonfinancial and financial state-owned enterprises.

In addition, in response to a decision by the Chinese Communist Party Central Committee (2017), the State Council is required to report annually to the National People's Congress, China's legislative body, on the management of state assets. This report, first issued in October 2018, also includes summary data on the magnitude of state assets (State Council 2018b).

Several important analytical studies of China's national balance sheet are based largely on the data sources outlined above. One of the first was sponsored by the Boyuan Foundation and led by Ma Jun, at the time the chief economist for Greater China at Deutsche Bank (Ma, Zhang, and Li 2012). In addition, Li Yang, a senior economist in the Chinese Academy of Social Sciences, led a group that has published two comprehensive studies of China's national balance sheet (Li, Zhang, and Chang 2013, 2015). Li and his coauthors also published two articles focusing on China's sovereign balance sheet, largely summarizing the analysis in their 2013 book (Li et al. 2012a, 2012b). Finally, the People's Bank of China, China's central bank, has published research on the Chinese government balance sheet (People's Bank of China 2016).

State-Owned Assets in International Perspective

State-owned assets in 2014 were valued at RMB227 trillion, disaggregated into the several categories shown in table A.1. RMB227 trillion is 3.6 times China's 2014 GDP of RMB63.6 trillion (National Bureau of Statistics of China 2016a, 21). At RMB116.2 trillion the assets of state-controlled nonfinancial enterprises are the single largest component. The second largest component is land, valued at RMB65.4 trillion.

These numbers make China an extreme outlier in terms of the value of state-owned nonfinancial assets relative to GDP. In 2014 the value of state-owned nonfinancial assets of RMB195 trillion (sum of the first, second, and fourth items in table A.1) was 3.1 times the value of GDP. To compare, an

Table A.1 State assets, 2014

Asset	Trillions of renminbi
Nonfinancial enterprises	116.2
Land resources	65.4
Financial sector	27.7
Administrative and public institutions	13.4
Government deposits at central bank	3.1
National social security fund	1.5
Total	227.3

Source: Li, Zhang, and Chang (2015).

IMF analysis of the nonfinancial assets on government balance sheets found that the average (median) ratio for 30 countries with reasonable data was 67 (50) percent of GDP and the highest ratio, for Latvia, was 180 percent (IMF 2013, 8).

China is an outlier primarily because of the large value of the assets of state-controlled enterprises and to a lesser extent the value of state-controlled land. These were equivalent to 125 and 70 percent, respectively, of GDP in 2014. Assets of Chinese state enterprises are predominantly buildings and machinery and equipment, with machinery and equipment accounting for the lion's share. Other countries in the IMF study do not report on assets of state companies; rather they separately report data on the value of state-owned buildings and structures and on the value of state-owned machinery and equipment. What share of the assets reported in these categories could be due to state-owned enterprises as opposed to government administrative units? For countries reporting disaggregated data, the value of state-owned machinery is typically around 2 to 3 percent of GDP; the highest is Russia at 5 percent. These low numbers suggest that state-owned machinery in the countries in the IMF study primarily comprises office equipment, vehicles, and so forth associated with government administration, not the telecommunication networks, steel mills, mining equipment, oil refineries, and so forth owned by state enterprises in China. Thus, in these other countries the value of state-owned buildings and structures must primarily reflect government ownership of offices for central and local government officials rather than factory structures owned by state-owned enterprises.[3] In China the value of state assets of administrative and public institutions in 2014 was RMB13.4 billion, about 20 percent of

---

3. For countries with disaggregated data, except Barbados, Colombia, Japan, and Slovenia, the value of state-owned dwellings constitutes a trivial share of the value of state-owned buildings and structures (IMF 2013, 41–43).

Table A.2 Assets of state nonfinancial enterprises, 2008–15
(billions of renminbi)

Year	Total	Agriculture	Industry and construction	Services
2008	41,622	368	20,973	21,970
2009	51,414	435	24,933	28,057
2010	64,021	523	28,723	34,776
2011	75,908	656	33,635	41,617
2012	89,489	772	37,686	51,030
2013	104,095	909	41,564	61,621
2014	118,472	1,041	45,273	72,158
2015	140,683	1,079	48,265	91,339

Note: For unknown reasons the sum of the three components for 2008 and 2009 exceeds the reported totals.

Source: Ministry of Finance (2016a, 388).

GDP. Presumably the largest component of these assets is buildings. Twenty percent of GDP is a smaller ratio than all the countries in the IMF study for which disaggregated data on state-owned buildings and structures are available.

The average value of state-owned land in the 13 countries in the IMF study for which these data are available is 21 percent of GDP. Only South Korea at 63 percent approaches the 70 percent level in China. In short, China is an outlier in terms of the value of state-owned nonfinancial assets relative to GDP primarily because of the large amount of assets of state-owned nonfinancial enterprises and secondarily because of the high value of state-owned land.

One of the main recommendations of this study is more efficient use of assets in state-owned nonfinancial enterprises, i.e., state firms in the primary sector, which includes agriculture, forestry, animal husbandry, and fisheries; secondary sector, which includes industry and construction; and tertiary sector, which includes services (excluding finance). As shown in table A.2, by 2015, these assets stood at RMB141 trillion, with roughly one-third controlled by state-owned industrial and construction firms and two-thirds by state-owned nonfinancial services firms. As a practical matter, state assets in the primary sector are tiny, so the study focuses almost exclusively on industry, construction, and services.

Note on Methodology

Interpretation of asset data in any economy depends on a firm understanding of how such data are compiled and maintained. For example, when land is recognized as an asset, does the valuation include subsoil assets, i.e., deposits of oil, minerals, and so forth? In China the value of state-owned land and resources excludes the value of subsoil assets (Li et al. 2012a, 9).

Are asset values measured at historical value, market value, or replacement cost? Historical cost, typically adjusted by deducting depreciation from the initial cost of the asset, is the easiest form of valuation but will understate the value of assets in periods of high inflation. Market valuation has obvious appeal, but market prices for some assets can be notoriously volatile. Replacement cost is typically used to value assets for which there is no market but estimating replacement cost is very resource intensive (IMF 2013, 35–36). The enterprise accounting standards in China require that most assets be valued at historical cost, adjusted for depreciation (Ministry of Finance 2006b). An exception is inventory, which must be valued at the lowest of either cost or realizable net value (Ministry of Finance 2006a).

In addition, it is important to know whether the reported aggregate value of enterprise assets is calculated by simply adding up the assets of all enterprises or measured on a consolidated basis. This is particularly important in China where dozens of group companies control, via ownership stakes, many subordinate firms. If the assets of all the subordinate firms are added to the assets of the group company, there will be substantial double counting. In 2014, for example, the sum of the assets of all state enterprises was almost 60 percent greater than consolidated assets.[4] The data in tables A.1 and A.2 are consolidated.

---

4. Data from SASAC obtained from Wind Financial Information.

Appendix B
Enterprise Subsidies

Disclosures by Chinese nonfinancial companies listed on the Shanghai and Shenzhen stock exchanges provide information on explicit, direct subsidies these companies receive from the state.[1] This appendix presents some of this information for 2,918 listed nonfinancial firms in 2015 and extrapolates the implications for the broader universe of Chinese firms.[2] This analysis has important implications for understanding official data on enterprise profits and losses, as well as calculations of return on assets, which are based on official data on profit and assets.

Direct, disclosed subsidies to listed nonfinancial companies in 2015 totaled RMB157 billion. These subsidies have grown substantially over time, from an amount equivalent to only 5 percent of listed firm profits prior to receiving subsidies in 2010 to almost 14 percent in 2015. The Chinese government provides many types of direct enterprise subsidies. Some, such as subsidies for research and development, energy conservation projects, and environmental projects, are well specified and received by firms in many industries. Other subsidies carry much more generic labels, making it difficult or impossible to determine why the government granted a subsidy to a specific firm. Subsidies

---

1. See the last paragraph of this appendix for a brief discussion of implicit subsidies, for example, when financial institutions write off nonperforming loans.

2. Unless otherwise specified, data in this appendix are from Wind Financial Information. The analysis is for listed nonfinancial companies in order to be comparable with aggregate profit data released by the Ministry of Finance, which also cover nonfinancial firms.

of this latter type are identified by labels such as sectoral subsidies, rebates of taxes and fees, enterprise development, and support subsidies.

A review of individual company disclosures and an analysis of aggregate data both show that reported direct subsidies are designed to promote specific government policies rather than simply keeping money-losing companies afloat. For example, in 2015, to promote the domestic production of shale gas, the government announced that it would offer a subsidy of RMB0.3 per cubic meter of shale gas extracted starting in 2016 and continuing through 2018. In another example, the government granted subsidies to Wanda Cinema Line Company Ltd., a listed subsidiary of the Dalian Wanda Group, of RMB122 million and RMB248 million, respectively, in 2015 and 2016 for constructing a film center, using digital equipment for movie screening, and other projects—all in line with the government's objective of developing the movie industry in China. Yet another example is Sinopec, the listed subsidiary of the China Petrochemical Corporation. Starting in 2011 the government began to provide subsidies to the firm to compensate for the gap between the price of its natural gas imports and the lower state-fixed domestic price that Sinopec charged to users. These subsidies, clearly designed to facilitate the shift away from coal-based energy, exceeded RMB10 billion in both 2014 and 2015 and are scheduled to continue through 2020. Similarly, state firms in industries with excess capacity are receiving subsidies for retraining laid-off workers and other expenses related to downsizing. China Aluminum Shareholding Company Limited, a listed arm of China Aluminum Corporation (Chalco), which received RMB1,770 million in various subsidies in 2015, may be an example.

Aggregate data also strongly suggest that direct subsidies are used primarily to promote government policy. Four observations support this view. First, the distribution of subsidies is far broader than would be required to simply offset the losses of firms that are unprofitable. In 2015, for example, 2,834 listed nonfinancial companies received subsidies of one sort or another; only 84 listed companies did not. Second, 2,391 listed firms, or more than four-fifths of these subsidized listed firms, were profitable even prior to receiving subsidies. Wanda Cinema Line Company is a good example of a profitable subsidized firm.[3] Its pretax, presubsidy profits in 2015 were RMB1,561 million. Third, this group of profitable but subsidized listed firms accounted for three-quarters of all subsidies received by listed nonfinancial firms; listed loss-making firms received the remaining one-quarter of all subsidies. Fourth, three-quarters of the 443 listed loss-making companies that received subsidies continued to make

---

3. The company subsequently changed its name to Wanda Film Holding Co. Ltd.

losses even after receiving subsidies; the subsidies fell short of the amount that would have been required to push these companies into the black. In about a quarter of the cases these subsidies were sufficient to convert losses into profits. This strongly suggests that the loss makers received subsidies because their activities supported government policy. In short, at least for listed companies, direct subsidies are not granted simply to offset losses, as is commonly believed.

In 2015 RMB111 billion, or 70 percent of the total subsidies to listed nonfinancial companies, went to listed state companies. Out of 966 listed state companies, only 32 did not receive subsidies. The absolute size of explicit, direct subsidies received by listed state firms is relatively small compared to the losses of state firms reflected in table 2.1, but only a tiny share of Chinese state firms is listed.[4]

We can explore how large these subsidies might be in the larger universe of state nonfinancial firms by assuming that the share of subsidies in pretax, presubsidy profits in listed state nonfinancial companies and in the broader universe of state nonfinancial companies is the same. On this assumption, in 2015 total subsidies received by all state nonfinancial companies, both listed and not listed, would have been about RMB543 billion, an amount just over a fifth of their reported profits.[5] We can then adjust the return on assets of these firms. Based on the data published by the Ministry of Finance (2016a, 378), the return on assets of all state firms in 2015 was 1.8 percent. After subtracting subsidies from reported profits, the "true" return on assets for state firms was 1.4 percent.

Almost all listed private nonfinancial companies also received subsidies so their profits, and probably the profits of the broader universe of private nonfinancial companies, also are overstated. But the degree of overstatement is smaller than for state companies. Subsidies received by listed state companies were 14.6 percent of their pretax, presubsidy profits, whereas subsidies to

---

4. In 2015 there were 291,263 legal person state-owned firms (National Bureau of Statistics of China 2016b, 22).

5. My analysis and calculations are based on data from Wind Financial Information on listed state nonfinancial firms and data from the Ministry of Finance on the profits of profitable state nonfinancial firms, the losses of loss-making state nonfinancial firms, and the profits of all state nonfinancial firms. It assumes that the distribution of profits among state firms not receiving subsidies, state firms receiving subsides but profitable prior to the subsidies, loss-making state firms profitable after subsidies, and loss-making state firms receiving subsidies but still loss-making after subsidies is the same as these shares in the universe of listed state companies. It next assumes that the extent of subsidies received by these classes of firms is the same as received by the same class of listed state firms.

listed private firms were only 10.4 percent of their pretax, presubsidy profits.[6] In short, the subsidies of state firms are about 40 percent larger, relative to profits.[7]

In addition to explicit, direct subsidies, state-owned enterprises are the beneficiaries of implicit subsidies that are not generally reported. These include writeoffs of nonperforming loans and the allocation of land and the supply of natural resources to state-owned companies at below market value. Adjusting for various types of implicit support, Lam and Schipke (2017, 316) estimate that total state subsidies for above-scale state industrial enterprises in 2015 were about 3 percent of GDP or RMB1.8 trillion, more than three times my estimate of explicit, direct subsidies of RMB543 billion, which includes subsidies to state-owned service enterprises.

---

6. In the Wind Financial Information database, the classification of firms includes 116 public firms (公众企业), a category not used by the National Bureau of Statistics of China, the Ministry of Finance, or other Chinese government agencies. According to Wind Financial Information, shareholding in these firms is so widely dispersed that there is no controlling shareholder. I believe these firms also should be regarded as private. Their subsidies were RMB4.9 billion, only 6.2 percent of their presubsidy, pretax profits. If we combine these firms with private firms to form a "true private" class of firms, subsidies as a share of presubsidy, pretax profits of this class were 9.7 percent.

7. Subsidies of state firms were 50 percent larger relative to presubsidy, pretax profits than the universe of "true private" firms analyzed in the previous note.

References

Anderson, Jon. 2016. *The Mystery of Productivity, The Mystery of Savings* (July 4). Emerging Advisors Group. Available by subscription only at www.emadvisorsgroup.com (accessed on July 15, 2017).

Anderson, Jon. 2017. *China: There Is No Reform Agenda (Part 1)* (August 20). Emerging Advisors Group. Available by subscription only at www.emadvisorsgroup.com (accessed on August 3, 2017).

Andrews, Dan, Muge Adalet McGowan, and Valentine Millot. 2017. *Confronting the Zombies: Policies for Productivity Revival.* Economic Policy Paper No. 21. Paris: Organization for Economic Cooperation and Development.

Bedford, Jason. 2018. *China Banks: Are NPLs Set to Surge?* (June 20). UBS Global Research.

Brandt, Loren, Chang-tai Hsieh, and Xiaodong Zhu. 2008. Growth and Structural Transformation in China. In *China's Great Economic Transformation*, ed. Loren Brandt and Thomas G. Rawski. Cambridge: Cambridge University Press.

Cai Fang, Albert Park, and Yaohui Zhao. 2008. The Chinese Labor Market in the Reform Era. In *China's Great Economic Transformation*, ed. Loren Brandt and Thomas G. Rawski. Cambridge: Cambridge University Press.

Chamon, Marcos, and Eswar Prasad. 2008. *Why Are Savings Rates of Urban Households in China Rising?* IMF Working Paper 08/145 (June). Washington: International Monetary Fund.

Chen, Sophia, and Lev Ratnovski. 2018. Can Credit Still Prop Up the Chinese Economy? VoxChina, February 18. Available at www.voxchina.org (accessed on March 4, 2018).

China Banking Society. 2011. *Almanac of China's Finance and Banking 2011.* Beijing: China Financial Publishing House.

China Banking Society. 2012. *Almanac of China's Finance and Banking 2012.* Beijing: China Financial Publishing House.

China Banking Society. 2013. *Almanac of China's Finance and Banking 2013.* Beijing: China Financial Publishing House.

China Banking Society. 2014. *Almanac of China's Finance and Banking 2014.* Beijing: China Financial Publishing House.

China Banking Society. 2015. *Almanac of China's Finance and Banking 2015.* Beijing: China Financial Publishing House.

China Banking Society. 2016. *Almanac of China's Finance and Banking 2016.* Beijing: China Financial Publishing House.

China Banking Society. 2018. *Almanac of China's Finance and Banking 2017.* Beijing: China Financial Publishing House.

Chinese Communist Party Central Committee. 2013. Resolution Concerning Some Major Issues in Comprehensively Deepening Reform (November 15). Beijing. Available at http://chinacopyrightandmedia.wordpress.com (accessed on November 18, 2013).

Chinese Communist Party Central Committee. 2017. Opinion on Establishing the System of State Council Reporting to the Standing Committee of the National People's Congress on the Situation with Respect to the Management of State Assets (December 30). Available at www.npc.gov.cn (accessed on October 28, 2018).

Chinese Communist Party Central Committee. 2018. Plan for Deepening the Reform of Party and State Structures (March 21). Beijing. Available at www.gov.cn (accessed on March 30, 2018).

Chinese Communist Party Central Committee and State Council. 2015. Guiding Opinion on Deepening the Reform of State-Owned Enterprises (September 13). Beijing. Available at www.gov.cn/ (accessed on August 21, 2017).

Chinese Communist Party Central Committee and State Council. 2016. Opinion on Improving Property Rights Protection: Protecting Property Rights According to the Law (November 27). Beijing. Available at www.gov.cn (accessed on March 5, 2018).

Chivakul, Mali, and W. Raphael Lam. 2015. *Assessing China's Corporate Vulnerabilities.* IMF Working Paper 15/72 (March). Washington: International Monetary Fund. Available at www.imf.org (accessed on June 15, 2015).

Chorzempa, Martin. 2018. Is the US Treasury Going Too Far in Protecting US Technology? Trade and Investment Policy Watch, October 23. Washington: Peterson Institute for International Economics. Available at https://piie.com/blogs/trade-investment-policy-watch (accessed on October 31, 2018).

Cline, William R. 2014. *Estimates of Fundamental Equilibrium Exchange Rates.* PIIE Policy Brief 14-16 (May). Washington: Peterson Institute for International Economics.

Cline, William R., and John Williamson. 2008. *New Estimates of Fundamental Equilibrium Exchange Rates.* PIIE Policy Brief 08-7 (July). Washington: Peterson Institute for International Economics.

Cui, Ernan. 2016. The Retirement Policy Conundrum. *China Economic Quarterly* 20, no. 3 (September): 44–48. GavekalDragonomics. Available at www.gavekal.com (accessed on January 2, 2018).

Davies, Howard, and Matevz Raskovic. 2018. *Understanding a Changing China: Key Issues for Business.* London and New York: Routledge.

Dollar, David, and Shang-Jin Wei. 2007. *Das (Wasted) Kapital: Firm Ownership and Investment Efficiency in China.* IMF Working Paper 07/9 (January). Washington: International Monetary Fund.

Economy, Elizabeth C. 2018. *The Third Revolution: Xi Jinping and the New Chinese State.* New York: Oxford University Press.

Garnaut, Ross, and Yiping Huang. 2006. Continued Rapid Growth and the Turning Point in China's Development. In *The Turning Point in China's Economic Development,* ed. Ross Garnaut and Ligang Song. Canberra: ANU Press.

Gatley, Thomas. 2015. Cash Hogs on the Loose (December 8). GavekalDragonomics. Available at https://research.gavekal.com (accessed on March 18, 2018).

Gatley, Thomas. 2017. The China Inc. Annual Report 2017 (August). GavekalDragonomics. Available at https://research.gavekal.com (accessed on March 14, 2018).

Gatley, Thomas. 2018. The Working Capital Heist (January 9). GavekalDragonomics Ideas. Available at www.gavekal.com (accessed on March 14, 2018).

Gerschenkron, Alexander. 1966. *Economic Backwardness in Historical Perspective: A Book of Essays.* Cambridge, MA: Belknap Press of Harvard University Press.

Goldstein, Morris, and Nicholas R. Lardy. 2009. *The Future of China's Exchange Rate Policy.* Policy Analyses in International Economics 87. Washington: Peterson Institute for International Economics.

Golley, Jane, Rod Tyers, and Yixiao Zhou. 2016. Contradiction in Chinese Fertility and Savings: Long-Run Domestic and Global Implications. In *Structural Change in China: Implications for Australia and the World,* ed. Iris Day and John Simon. Sydney: Reserve Bank of Australia.

Guo Tongxin. 2017a. Reform Brings Forth an Acceleration in the Continuous Expansion of China's Employment (March 29). Available at www.stats.gov.cn (accessed on April 19, 2007).

Guo Tongxin. 2017b. Steadily Strive to Achieve Success; Reform Achieves New Good Results (June 8). Available at www.stats.gov.cn (accessed on June 12, 2017).

Hau, Harald, Yi Huang, Hongzhe Shan, and Zixia Sheng. 2017. Techfin at Ant Financial: Credit Market Completion and Its Growth Effect. Unpublished manuscript (December 19).

Hsieh, Chang-tai, and Peter Klenow. 2009. Misallocation and Manufacturing TFP in China and India. *Quarterly Journal of Economics* CXXIV, no. 4 (November):1403–48.

Hsieh, Chang-tai, and Zhen (Michael) Song. 2015. *Grasp the Large, Let Go of the Small: The Transformation of the State Sector in China.* NBER Working Paper 21006 (March). Cambridge, MA: National Bureau of Economic Research. Available at www.nber.org/papers/w21006 (accessed on June 13, 2018).

Hubbard, Paul. 2014. *Asiaphoria and Asiaphobia?* East Asia Forum (December 14). Available at www.eastasiaforum.org (accessed on December 30, 2014).

IFC (International Finance Corporation). 2007. *Reforming Collateral Laws and Registries: International Best Practices and the Case of China.* Washington. Available at www.ifc.org (accessed on February 18, 2014).

IMF (International Monetary Fund). 2011. *The People's Republic of China: 2011 Article IV Consultation—Staff Report* (July). Washington: Available at www.imf.org (accessed on July 21, 2011).

IMF (International Monetary Fund). 2013. *Another Look at Governments' Balance Sheets: The Role of Nonfinancial Assets.* IMF Working Paper 13/95 (May). Washington. Available at www.imf.org (accessed on January 13, 2017).

IMF (International Monetary Fund). 2015. *The People's Republic of China: 2015 Article IV Consultation—Staff Report* (August). Washington. Available at www.imf.org (accessed on August 15, 2015).

IMF (International Monetary Fund). 2016a. *The People's Republic of China: 2016 Article IV Consultation—Staff Report* (August). Washington. Available at www.imf.org (accessed on August 14, 2016).

IMF (International Monetary Fund). 2016b. *World Economic Outlook* (October). Washington: Available at www.imf.org (accessed on June 14, 2017).

IMF (International Monetary Fund). 2016c. *The People's Republic of China—Selected Issues* (August). Washington. Available at www.imf.org (accessed on August 25, 2016).

IMF (International Monetary Fund). 2016d. *Regional Economic Outlook: Asia and Pacific* (May). Washington. Available at www.imf.org (accessed on August 24, 2017).

IMF (International Monetary Fund). 2017a. *The People's Republic of China: 2017 Article IV Consultation—Staff Report* (August). Washington. Available at www.imf.org (accessed on August 15, 2017).

IMF (International Monetary Fund). 2017b. *The People's Republic of China—Selected Issues* (August). Washington. Available at www.imf.org (accessed on August 15, 2017).

IMF (International Monetary Fund). 2017c. *World Economic Outlook: Seeing Sustainable Growth* (October). Washington. Available at www.imf.org (accessed on October 16).

IMF (International Monetary Fund). 2017d. *The People's Republic of China: Financial System Stability Assessment* (October 24). Washington. Available at www.imf.org (accessed on December 6, 2017).

IMF (International Monetary Fund). 2018. *The People's Republic of China: 2018 Article IV Consultation—Staff Report* (July). Washington. Available at www.imf.org (accessed on July 27, 2018).

Jiang Zemin. 1997. Report to the Chinese Communist Party's 15th National Congress (September 12). Available at http://cpc.people.com (accessed on July 31, 2017).

Kozul-Wright, Richard, and Daniel Poon. 2017. Learning from China's Industrial Strategy. Project Syndicate, April 28. Available at www.project-syndicate.org (accessed on November 16, 2018).

Kroeber, Arthur. 2016. Making Sense of the Economic Policy Mess. *China Economic Quarterly* 19, no. 2 (June): 3–6. Available at www.gavekal.com (accessed on July 9, 2018).

Lam, W. Raphael, and Alfred Schipke. 2017. State-Owned Enterprise Reform. In *Modernizing China: Investing in Soft Infrastructure*, ed. W. Raphael Lam, Markus Rodlauer, and Alfred Schipke. Washington: International Monetary Fund.

Lam, W. Raphael, Alfred Schipke, Yuyan Tan, and Zhibo Tan. 2017. *Resolving China's Zombies: Tackling Debt and Raising Productivity* (November). IMF Working Paper 17/266. Washington: International Monetary Fund. Available at www.imf.org (accessed on November 28, 2017).

Lardy, Nicholas R. 1998. *China's Unfinished Economic Revolution*. Washington: Brookings Institution Press.

Lardy, Nicholas R. 2002. *Integrating China into the Global Economy*. Washington: Brookings Institution Press.

Lardy, Nicholas R. 2003. The Case of China. In *Financial Liberalization and the Economic Crisis in Asia*, ed. Chung H. Lee. London: RoutledgeCurzon.

Lardy, Nicholas R. 2012. *Sustaining China's Economic Growth after the Global Financial Crisis*. Washington: Peterson Institute for International Economics.

Lardy, Nicholas R. 2014. *Markets over Mao: The Rise of Private Business in China*. Washington: Peterson Institute for International Economics.

Lardy, Nicholas R. 2016. The Changing Role of the Private Sector in China. In *Structural Change in China: Implications for Australia and the World*. Sydney: Reserve Bank of Australia.

Leutert, Wendy. 2016. State-Owned Enterprise Mergers: Will Less Be More? *China Analysis* (November): 2–5. European Council on Foreign Relations. Available at www.ecfr.eu (accessed on April 16, 2017).

Li, Hongbin, Prashant Loyalka, Scott Rozelle, and Binzhen Wu. 2017. Human Capital and China's Future Growth. *Journal of Economic Perspectives* 31, no. 1 (Winter): 25–47.

Li Keqiang. 2017. *2017 Government Work Report* (March 5). Beijing. Available at http:// english.gov.cn (accessed on March 13, 2017).

Li Yang, Zhang Xiaojing, Chang Xin, Tang Duoduo, and Li Cheng. 2012a. China's Sovereign Balance Sheet and Its Risk Assessment. *Economic Research* no. 6: 4–19.

Li Yang, Zhang Xiaojing, Chang Xin, Tang Duoduo, and Li Cheng. 2012b. China's Sovereign Balance Sheet and Its Risk Assessment. *Economic Research* no. 7: 4–21.

Li Yang, Zhang Xiaojing, and Chang Xin. 2013. *China's National Balance Sheet 2013: Theory, Methodology, and Risk Evaluation*. Beijing: China Social Sciences Publishing House.

Li Yang, Zhang Xiaojing, and Chang Xin. 2015. *China's National Balance Sheet 2015: Leverage Readjustment and Risk Management*. Beijing: Social Sciences Publishing House.

Lin, Justin Yifu. 2013. Long Live China's Boom (August 5). Available at www.project-syndicate.org (accessed on January 14, 2015).

Lin, Justin Yifu, and Zhongkai Shen. 2018. Reform and Development Strategy. In *China's 40 Years of Reform and Development, 1978–2018*, ed. Ross Garnaut, Ligang Song, and Cai Fang. Canberra: ANU Press.

Liu Qiao. 2016. *Corporate China 2.0: The Great Shakeup*. New York: Palgrave Macmillan.

Ljungqvist, Alexander, Donghua Chen, Dequan Jiang, Haitian Lu, and Mingming Zhou. 2015. *State Capitalism vs. Private Enterprise*. NBER Working Paper 20930 (February). Cambridge, MA: National Bureau of Economic Research. Available at www.nber.org/papers/w20930 (accessed on June 13, 2018).

Ma Zhun, Zhang Xiaorong, and Li Zhiguo. 2012. *A Study of China's National Balance Sheet*. Beijing: Social Sciences Publishing House.

McKinsey Global Institute. 2015. *The China Effect on Global Innovation* (July). Available at www.mckinsey.com/mgi (accessed on April 25, 2017).

McMahon, Dinny. 2018. *China's Great Wall of Debt: Shadow Banks, Ghost Cities, Massive Loans, and the End of the Chinese Miracle*. Boston and New York: Houghton Mifflin Harcourt.

Ministry of Education Finance Office and National Bureau of Statistics, Social, Scientific, and Cultural Affairs Statistical Office. 2014. *China Educational Finance Statistical Yearbook*. Beijing: China Statistics Press.

Ministry of Finance. 2006a. *Enterprise Accounting Rule No. 1—Inventories* (February 15). Beijing. Available at http://kjs.mof.gov.cn (accessed on June 22, 2018).

Ministry of Finance. 2006b. *Enterprise Accounting Rule No. 4—Fixed Assets* (February 15). Beijing. Available at http://kjs.mof.gov.cn (accessed on June 22, 2018).

Ministry of Finance. 2011. *Report on the Implementation of the Central and Local Budgets for 2010 and on the Draft Central and Local Budgets for 2011* (March 5). Beijing. Available at http://English.gov.cn (accessed on December 14, 2016).

Ministry of Finance. 2015. *Finance Yearbook of China 2015*. Beijing: China Financial Magazine Publishing House.

Ministry of Finance. 2016a. *Finance Yearbook of China 2016*. Beijing: China Financial Magazine Publishing House.

Ministry of Finance. 2016b. *The Economic Situation in the 12 Months of 2015 of State-Owned and State-Controlled Enterprises* (January 26). Beijing. Available at www.zcgls.mof.gov.cn (accessed on December 8, 2017).

Ministry of Finance. 2017a. *The Economic Situation in the 12 Months of 2016 of State-Owned and State-Controlled Enterprises* (January 26). Beijing. Available at www.zcgls.mof.gov.cn (accessed on December 8, 2017).

Ministry of Finance. 2017b. *Finance Yearbook of China 2017*. Beijing: China Financial Magazine Publishing House.

Ministry of Human Resources and Social Security. 2017a. *Next Year the Unification of the National Old Age Pension System Will Take a First Step: Carrying Out the Central Adjustment System* (November 11). Beijing. Available at www.mohrss.gov.cn (accessed on January 12, 2018).

Ministry of Human Resources and Social Security. 2017b. *Statistical Report on the Development of Human Resource and Social Security Undertakings in 2016* (May 31). Beijing. Available at www.mohrss.gov.cn (accessed on January 12, 2018).

Minzner, Carl. 2018. *End of an Era: How China's Authoritarian Revival Is Undermining Its Rise*. New York: Oxford University Press.

Nabar, Malhar. 2011. *Targets, Interest Rates, and Household Saving in Urban China* (September). IMF Working Paper 11/223. Washington: International Monetary Fund. Available at www.imf.org (accessed on June 13, 2017).

National Bureau of Statistics of China. 1999. *China Statistical Yearbook 1999*. Beijing: China Statistics Press.

National Bureau of Statistics of China. 2001. *China Statistical Yearbook 2001*. Beijing: China Statistics Press.

National Bureau of Statistics of China. 2006. *China Statistical Yearbook 2006*. Beijing: China Statistics Press.

National Bureau of Statistics of China. 2007. *China Statistical Yearbook 2007*. Beijing: China Statistics Press.

National Bureau of Statistics of China. 2008. *China Statistical Yearbook 2008*. Beijing: China Statistics Press.

National Bureau of Statistics of China. 2010a. *China Statistical Yearbook 2010*. Beijing: China Statistics Press.

National Bureau of Statistics of China. 2010b. *China Economic Census Yearbook 2008*. Beijing: China Statistics Press.

National Bureau of Statistics of China. 2012. *China Statistical Yearbook 2012*. Beijing: China Statistics Press.

National Bureau of Statistics of China. 2013. *China Statistical Yearbook 2013*. Beijing: China Statistics Press.

National Bureau of Statistics of China. 2014. *China Statistical Yearbook of the Tertiary Industry 2014*. Beijing: China Statistics Press.

National Bureau of Statistics of China. 2015. *China Statistical Yearbook 2015*. Beijing: China Statistics Press.

National Bureau of Statistics of China. 2016a. *China Statistical Abstract 2016*. Beijing: China Statistics Press.

National Bureau of Statistics of China. 2016b. *China Statistical Yearbook 2016*. Beijing: China Statistics Press.

National Bureau of Statistics of China. 2017a. *Preliminary Accounting of China's GDP in the Fourth Quarter and the Whole Year of 2016* (January 21). Beijing. Available at www.stats.gov.cn (accessed on January 23, 2017).

National Bureau of Statistics of China. 2017b. *Statistical Report on China's Economic and Social Development in 2016* (February 28). Beijing. Available at www.stats.gov.cn (accessed on February 28, 2017).

National Bureau of Statistics of China. 2017c. *China Statistical Abstract 2017*. Beijing: China Statistics Press.

National Bureau of Statistics of China. 2017d. *Report on Final Verified 2015 GDP* (January 9). Beijing. Available at www.stats.gov.cn (accessed on January 9, 2017).

National Bureau of Statistics of China. 2017e. *China Statistical Yearbook 2017*. Beijing: China Statistics Press.

National Bureau of Statistics of China. 2017f. *Total Profits of Above-Scale Industrial Enterprises Increased by 8.5 Percent in 2016 Compared with the Previous Year* (January 26). Beijing. Available at www.stats.gov.cn (accessed on January 30, 2017).

National Bureau of Statistics of China. 2018a. *The 2017 Economic Situation Steadily Improved, Better Than Expected* (January 18). Beijing. Available at www.stats.gov.cn (accessed on January 18, 2018).

National Bureau of Statistics of China. 2018b. *Statistical Report on China's Economic and Social Development in 2017* (February 28). Beijing. Available at www.stats.gov.cn (accessed on March 3, 2018).

National Bureau of Statistics of China. 2018c. *Profits of Above-Scale Chinese Industrial Enterprises Rose 21 Percent in 2017* (January 26). Beijing. Available at www.stats.gov.cn (accessed on January 26, 2018).

National Bureau of Statistics of China, Comprehensive Office. 2018. *China's Development Is a Global Opportunity* (April 12). Beijing. Available at www.stats.gov.cn (accessed on April 17, 2018).

National Bureau of Statistics and Ministry of Human Resources and Social Security. 2018. *China Labour Statistics Yearbook 2017*. Beijing: China Statistics Press.

National Development and Reform Commission. 2016. *Outline for China's 13th Five-Year Program for National Economic and Social Development* (March 17). Available at http://en.ndrc.gov.cn (accessed on March 9, 2018).

National People's Congress. 2007. Labour Contract Law of the PRC, adopted by the 28th Meeting of the Standing Committee of the 10th National People's Congress, Beijing, June 29. Available at www.npc.gov.cn (accessed on May 27, 2018).

Naughton, Barry. 2016a. State Enterprise Reform: Missing in Action. *China Economic Quarterly* 20, no. 2 (June): 15–21. GavekalDragonomics. Available at www.gavekal.com (accessed on May 26, 2018).

Naughton, Barry. 2016b. Restructuring and Reform. In *Structural Change in China: Implications for Australia and the World*. Sydney: Reserve Bank of Australia.

Naughton, Barry. 2017. Is China Socialist? *Journal of Economic Perspectives* 31, no. 1 (Winter): 3–24.

Naughton, Barry. 2018. State Enterprise Reform Today. In *China's 40 Years of Reform and Development, 1978–2018*, ed. Ross Garnaut, Ligang Song, and Cai Fang. Canberra: ANU Press.

Noland, Marcus, and Howard Pack. 2003. *Industrial Policy in an Era of Globalization: Lessons from Asia*. Washington: Institute for International Economics.

Pei Minxin. 1998. The Political Economy of Banking Reforms in China, 1993–1997. *Journal of Contemporary China* 7, no. 17 (July): 321–50.

People's Bank of China. 2016. *The Compilation and Analysis of Chinese Government Balance Sheet*. Beijing. Available at https://www.bis.org/ifc/events/ifc_8thconf/ifc_8thconf_4c2pap.pdf (accessed on February 24, 2017).

People's Bank of China. 2017. *Balance Sheet of the Monetary Authority* (July 20). Beijing. Available at www.pbc.gov (accessed on August 9, 2017).

People's Bank of China. Quarterly. *Statistical Report on China's Microfinance Companies*. Beijing. Various issues. Available at www.pbc.gov (accessed on March 14, 2018).

People's Bank of China Monetary Policy Analysis Small Group. 2017. *Report on Implementation of Monetary Policy, Fourth Quarter 2016* (February 17). Beijing. Available at www.pbc.gov.cn (accessed on February 17, 2017).

Perkins, Dwight H., and Thomas G. Rawski. 2008. Forecasting China's Economic Growth to 2025. In *China's Great Economic Transformation*, ed. Loren Brandt and Thomas G. Rawski. Cambridge: Cambridge University Press.

Pettis, Michael. 2016a. Rebalancing, Wealth Transfers, and the Growth of Chinese Debt (June 22). Available at www.talkmarkets.com/contributor/michael-pettis/blog (accessed on October 30, 2018).

Pettis, Michael. 2016b. The Impact in China and Abroad of Slowing Growth (October 2). Available at http://carnegieendowment.org/chinafinancialmarkets (accessed on December 30, 2016).

Pettis, Michael. 2016c. China: Choosing More Debt, More Unemployment, or Transfers (November 20). Available at http://carnegieendowment.org/chinafinancialmarkets (accessed on December 30, 2012).

Pettis, Michael. 2017. My Reading of the FT's "Glimpse of China's Economic Future" (January 6). Available at http://carnegieendowment.org/chinafinancialmarkets (accessed on January 18, 2017).

Posen, Adam S. 1998. *Restoring Japan's Economic Growth*. Washington: Institute for International Economics.

Pritchett, Lant, and Lawrence H. Summers. 2014. *Asiaphoria Meets Regression to the Mean*. NBER Working Paper 20573 (October). Cambridge, MA: National Bureau of Economic Research. Available at www.nber.org/papers/w20573 (accessed on May 15, 2016).

Rawski, Thomas G. 2017. Growth, Upgrading and Excess Cost in China's Electric Power Sector. Unpublished manuscript.

Rodrik, Dani. 2011. *The Future of Economic Convergence*. HKS Faculty Research Working Paper Series. Harvard University. Available at http://web/hks/harvard.edu (accessed on August 23, 2017).

SASAC (State-Owned Assets Supervision and Administration Commission). 2011. *China's State-Owned Assets Supervision and Administration Yearbook 2011*. Beijing: China Economic Publishing House.

SASAC (State-Owned Assets Supervision and Administration Commission), Management Office of the Central Party Organization Department, Ministry of Education, Ministry of Finance, Ministry of Human Resources and Social Insurance, and Public Health and Family Planning Commission. 2017. *Guiding Opinion Concerning Deepening Reform of Educational and Health Organizations Run by State Enterprises* (August 25). Beijing. Available at www.gov.cn (accessed on August 25, 2017).

Song Ligang. 2018. State-Owned Enterprise Reform in China: Past, Present and Prospects. In *China's 40 Years of Reform and Development, 1978–2018*, ed. Ross Garnaut, Ligang Song, and Cai Fang. Canberra: ANU Press.

State Administration of Foreign Exchange International Balance of Payments Analysis Small Group. 2017. *Report on China's International Balance of Payments in 2016* (March 30). Beijing. Available at www.safe.gov.cn (accessed on April 10, 2017).

State Administration of Taxation. 2016. *Replacement of the Business Tax by the Value-Added Tax in 2016 Will Reduce the Scale of Taxation by More than RMB500 Billion* (December 23). Beijing. Available at www.chinatax.gov.cn (accessed on August 22, 2017).

State Council. 2015a. *Made in China 2025* (May 8). Beijing. Available at www.gov.cn (accessed on June 21, 2016).

State Council. 2015b. *Opinion on the Development of the Mixed Ownership Economy by State Enterprises* (September 23). Beijing. Available at www.gov.cn (accessed on July 31, 2017).

State Council. 2016a. *Guiding Opinion on the Restructuring and Reorganization of Central State-Owned Enterprises* (July 26). Beijing. Available at www.gov.cn (accessed on August 21, 2017).

State Council. 2016b. *Opinion on Actively and Reliably Lowering the Leverage Ratio of Enterprises* (September 22). Beijing. Available at www.gov.cn (accessed on June 26, 2018).

State Council. 2017a. *Guiding Opinions on Further Perfecting the Legal Governing Structure of State-Owned Enterprises* (April 24). Beijing. Available at www.gov.cn (accessed on June 16, 2017).

State Council. 2017b. *Notice on Reform Work Implementation Methods for the Corporatization of Central Enterprises* (July 18). Beijing. Available at www.sasac.gov.cn (accessed on July 27, 2017).

State Council. 2018a. *Notice Concerning the Establishment of the Central Adjustment Mechanism for the Basic Old Age Retirement Fund of Enterprise Workers and Staff* (May 30). Beijing. Available at www.gov.cn (accessed on June 14, 2018).

State Council. 2018b. *Comprehensive Report on the Situation with Respect to the Management of State Assets in 2017* (October 24, 2018). Beijing. Available at http://pkulaw.cn (accessed on October 26, 2018).

State Council Information Office. 2017. *Development of China's Public Health as an Essential Element of Human Rights* (September 29). Beijing. Available at http://english.gov.cn/archive/whitepaper/2017/09/29content (accessed on October 16, 2017).

State Council Second National Economic Census Leading Small Group Office. 2010. *China Economic Census Yearbook 2008*. Beijing: China Statistics Press.

Stent, James. 2017. Chinese Banks Are Better Than You Think. *China Economic Quarterly* 21, no. 3 (September): 37–41. GavekalDragonomics. Available at www.gavekal.com.

Supreme People's Court. 2017. *Circular on the Situation of Bankruptcy Trial Work* (February 25). Beijing. Available at www.court.gov.cn (accessed on January 29, 2018).

Tan Yuyan, Yiping Huang, and Wing Thye Woo. 2016. Zombie Firms and the Crowding-Out of Private Investment in China. *Asian Economic Papers* 15, no. 3: 32–55.

Tidrick, Gene. 2012. China's State-Owned Enterprises in International Perspective. Unpublished manuscript (September).

USTR (United States Trade Representative). 2011. *2011 National Trade Estimate Report on Foreign Trade Barriers*. Washington.

US-China Economic and Security Review Commission. 2012. *2012 Report to Congress*. Washington: US Government Printing Office.

Wolf, Martin. 2016. The Great Stall. *American Interest* (February 8). Available at www.the-american-interest.com (accessed on February 9, 2016).

World Bank. 1996. *China: Reform of State-Owned Enterprises*. Washington.

World Bank. 1997. *Old Age Security: Pension Reform in China*. Washington.

World Bank. 2008. *Mid-Term Evaluation of China's 11th Five-Year Plan*. Washington.

World Bank. 2012. *China 2030: Building a Modern, Harmonious, and Creative High-Income Society* (Conference Edition). Washington.

World Bank. 2016. *Global Economic Prospects: Divergences and Risks* (June). Washington. Available at www.worldbank.org (accessed on August 24, 2017).

World Bank. 2018a. *Global Economic Prospects: Broad-Based Upturn, but for How Long?* (January). Washington. Available at www.worldbank.org (accessed on January 25, 2018).

World Bank. 2018b. *Global Economic Prospects: The Turn of the Tide?* (June). Washington. Available at www.worldbank.org (accessed on June 6, 2018).

World Bank. 2018c. *China Economic Update: Investing in High-Quality Growth* (May). Washington. Available at www.worldbank.org (accessed on August 10, 2018).

World Bank, Institute of Developing Economies (a unit of the Japanese External Trade Organization), Organization for Economic Cooperation and Development, Research Center of Global Value Chains (based at the University of International Business and Economics in Beijing), and World Trade Organization. 2017. *Measuring and Analyzing the Impact of GVCs on Economic Development*. Washington.

WTO (World Trade Organization). 2017. *World Trade Statistical Review 2017* (July). Geneva. Available at www.wto.org (accessed on September 7, 2017).

Wu, Harry X. 2017. China's Institutional Impediment to Productivity Growth: An Industry-Origin Growth Accounting Approach. Unpublished manuscript (April 25).

Wübbeke, Jost, Mirjam Meissner, Max J. Zenglein, Jaqueline Ives, and Björn Conrad. 2016. *Made in China 2025: the making of a high-tech superpower and consequences for industrial countries.* Merics Papers on China No. 2 (December) Available at https://merics.org (accessed on October 30, 2018).

Xi Jinping. 2017. Secure a Decisive Victory in Building a Moderately Prosperous Society in All Respects and Strive for the Great Success of Socialism with Chinese Characteristics for a New Era (October 18). Beijing. Available at http://news.xinhuanet.com/english/special/2017-11/03/c_136725942.htm (accessed on November 3, 2017).

Xie Yanmei. 2017. *China Unicom's Mixed-Ownership Mixup* (August 25). GavekalDragonomics. Available at www.gavekal.com.

Zhao Yaohui, and Xu Jianguo. 2001. Incentive Problems in China's Urban Pension Reform. *China Economic Quarterly* 1, no. 1 (October): 193–206.

Zimmerman, James M. 2005. *China Law Deskbook.* Chicago: American Bar Association Publishing.

Index

Bank of England, quantitative easing
program, 128
bank profits, 95, 116
bank regulators, authority of, 116
bankruptcy, 103–104, 103n
bankrupt firms, liquidation of, 100, 104
banks
allocation of funds, 6
capture of smaller by local officials, 96,
116
credit to state-owned enterprises, 20
facing financial repression, 36
foreign, 96
forgiving loans in exchange for equity, 93
lending to state-owned enterprises, 41
not actually owning equity, 93n
not imposing hard budget constraints, 63
not lending to small private firms, 64
obtaining more accurate information on,
95
proceedings against creditors prior to
2007, 104
rewarding to report nonperforming loans,
95–96
barriers to entry, reducing, 100–101
"basket of goods" approach, comparing
economic performance, 4
Beijing-Shanghai route, for high-speed passenger rail, 15, 16
Belt and Road Initiative, 122
Benchmark interest rate, on one-year loans
(January 1990–November 2017), 67f
board of directors, 82, 97
borrowers, leverage ratio of, 59, 61, 61f
borrowing, by state-owned enterprises, 59
business tax, 39, 115
"buy China" policy, 17

Canyon Bridge equity fund, 87n
capital
allocating, 49–50, 51b, 75–76
flows within large state and private group
companies, 75
formation, overstatement of, 20n
lower cost of, 64–66
misallocating for state-owned enterprises,
77

preferential access to, 64
reallocating to reduce dispersion, 48
capital goods, demand for, 64, 66
capital markets, encouraging more efficient,
6
capital-scarce economy, China remaining,
51b
capital stock, 44, 51b
catchup pattern, for poor countries, 44
Central Asia Pipeline of PetroChina, 87n
central bank. *See* People's Bank of China
(central bank)
Central Economic Work Conference in
December 2016, 83
Central Huijin, largest state-owned banks
controlled by, 115
Chile, sending copper exports to China, 9
China
assets, 133–37
catch-up potential, 47f
comparing with Japan, 119
convergence potential, 43–80
economic progress, 7
economic slowdown, 11
employment in state-owned enterprises,
123n
global economic role, 8–10
growth
began at an extremely low level of per
capita income, 47
consequences for other economies, 10
likely to slow due to resurgence in the
role of the state, 2
powering worldwide economic
expansion, 1
slower inflicting economic damage
on global GDP growth and on Asian
countries, 9
improving quality of labor, 24
most leveraged corporate sector, 59
per capita GDP compared to the US, 46
potential economic growth, 3
reduced its tariffs unilaterally, 83, 86
slowdown caused by transitory factors, 3
super rapid growth extending 40 years, 26
China Aluminum Shareholding Company
Limited, 140

China Banking and Insurance Regulatory Commission, 95, 95n

China Banking Regulatory Commission (CBRC), 95, 95n

China central bank. *See* People's Bank of China (central bank)

China Insurance Regulatory Commission (CIRC), 95n

China Investment Corporation, 115

China National Offshore Oil Corporation (CNOOC), 99, 101, 101n

China National Petroleum Corporation (CNPC), 99, 101, 101n

China Oilfield Services Ltd, 101n

China Petrochemical Corporation (Sinopec), 101, 140

China Petroleum and Chemical Corporation (Sinopec), 99

China Reform Holdings, 87n

China Securities Regulatory Commission, 106

China Statistical Yearbook of the Tertiary Industry (National Bureau of Statistics), 134

China Tower, 87n

China Unicom, 91, 92

China United Network Communications, 92n

Chinese Communist Party
committees enhancing the role of, 20
control of all aspects of China, 21
Organization Department of the Chinese Communist Party, 97
state-owned enterprises essential to, 122

Civil Procedure Law (1991), 104

CNIC Corporation, 87n

CNOOC. *See* China National Offshore Oil Corporation (CNOOC)

CNPC. *See* China National Petroleum Corporation (CNPC)

coal-based energy, subsidies facilitating the shift away from, 140

Cobb-Douglas production function, 43–44

Commercial Bank Law (1995), 93n, 104

commercial enterprises, 94n

commercial state enterprises, 94, 95

commodity exporters/importers, 10

Communist Party. *See* Chinese Communist Party

Company Law of 1994, 81, 82

competition
absence of, driving up costs and reducing profits, 101
in China's domestic market, 83
between fully private and publicly owned banks, 96
increase in, resulting from lower trade barriers, 83
increasing by licensing new shareholding banks and city commercial banks, 104
increasing within each economic sector, 99
opening of the economy to external, 16

conditional approach, predicting China's growth from 2013 through 2033, 26

consolidated assets, versus sum of assets, 137

construction and engineering companies, more leveraged outside China, 122

consumption, as a share of GDP steadily rising, 120

contract workers, hired by labor dispatching units, 124

convergence
hypothesis
analyzing growth potential over the medium term, 44–45
on China's economic growth potential, 4
on poor countries growing faster, 44
potential for China, 78–80

corporate board, 82, 97

corporate governance program, 97

corporate loans, 105–106

corporatization
gradual and long-term nature of, 82
of state-owned industrial enterprises, 84t–85t
of traditional state-owned enterprises, 81–86

corporatized state-owned enterprises, transparency of, 97

corporatized state-owned industrial enterprises, assets controlled by, 83

courts, discretion in bankruptcy cases, 104

credit
    accompanied by slower growth, 121
    fast growth of, 9
    growing more rapidly than GDP, 22
    growth through expanded lending of local
        banks, 115
    increase in domestic relative to GDP, 59
    misallocation to least efficient, loss-making
        state firms, 22
    provided by the state-owned banking
        system, 2
    terms allowing expansion of underper-
        forming state-owned enterprises, 78
credit-financed stimulus program, 17, 79
creditor rights, insecure prior to 2007, 104
creditors, legal protection for, 104
credit to GDP ratio, 59
creditworthiness, metrics of, 61
crude oil, price of, 66, 68
currency. *See also* renminbi
    manipulation, 13
    undervaluation, 38
current growth, not predicting future
    growth, 25

debt, rising burden of China's, 21–22
debt at risk, defined, 63
debt burden, rising, 11t, 22
debt servicing capacity, 22
debt-to-equity program, 97
debt-to-equity swaps, 93–94, 94n
deceleration, in growth as long overdue, 26
deleveraging, headwinds against achieving,
    127
demand side factors, driving the rebalancing
    process, 32–38
demographic dividend, 23, 34–35
demographics, 32, 34
demography, 11t, 23–25
Deng Xiaoping, 1–2, 124
dependency ratio, 34–35
deposits, lower interest rates reducing house-
    hold income, 35
depreciating currency, effect of, 11
depreciation funds, invested to offset real
    depreciation, 90n

developed and developing economies, gap
    between, 45
developed countries, 43, 44–45
developing countries, growth process, 25
developing economies, grew faster than
    developed economies, 45
digital equipment, for movie screening, 140
direct enterprise subsidies, 53, 139–40
disposable income, 31n, 33f
dollar depreciation, 12
domestic banks, 96
domestic convergence, potential for, 78–80
domestic credit, ratio to GDP in China, 1
domestic debt, 21, 22, 124
domestic developments, reduced China's
    trade surpluses, 3
domestic economic policy, slowing pace of
    economic reform, 27
domestic economic reform, slowing pace
    of, 4
domestic merger and acquisition activity,
    2007, 2015, and 2016, 102t
domestic money supply, increased by pur-
    chases of foreign exchange, 36
domestic saving-investment imbalance,
    rising, 11
domestic savings, too large to be absorbed, 9
Dongbei Special Steel Group Co., 6, 103,
    103n
doubtful loans, 94n

EBIT (earnings before interest and taxes),
    50n
economic correction, China overdue for, 9
economic expansion, after the global finan-
    cial crisis, 10
economic growth
    forces determining China's current pace
        of, 120
    rapid, as a factor in the rebalancing
        process, 32
    rebalancing of the sources of, 120
economic imbalances, severe, 9
economic liberalization, 20
economic performance
    metrics
        for judging, 51b

for measuring dispersion in, 50, 51*b*
economic rebalancing, 28
economic reform. *See also* reform
  program proposed, 3
  prospects for further, 119–29
  slowing pace of, 16, 41
  sustaining China's growth, 119
economic slowdown, after the global financial crisis, 7–41
economy, immensity of China's, 7
educational attainment, in countries, 24
educational institutions, state enterprises
  running, 72
electricity system, dominated by massive
  state-owned enterprises, 77
electric power industry firms, overinvestment
  and excess capacity, 77
electric power output, state-owned enterprises retaining a near monopoly, 76*n*
emerging-market and developing economies,
  potential growth of, 45–46
employee share-holding scheme, in China
  Unicom, 92
employment, maintaining, 117
Engel's law, 32
enterprise accounting standards, 137
"enterprises owned by the whole people,"
  decline in the number of, 82
enterprise subsidies, 139–42
entrepreneurs, discouraged from investing,
  41
equity, equal to total assets minus total
  liabilities, 59
European Central Bank, 127–28
European Union, 129
exchange rate, 13, 38
exchange rate policy, 8, 12, 13
expenditure perspective, on rebalancing, 28
Export Control Reform Act (US), 8
exports, 14
external surplus, 12, 13

fertility, 23, 34
50:50 joint ventures, between state-owned
  enterprises and foreign firms, 19*n*
financial instability, leadership's fear of, 124

financial institutions, misallocation of
  capital, 75, 78
financial intermediation, share of private
  investment, 40*f*
financial liberalization program, 96
financial performance indicators, 117
financial reforms, 95–96, 97
financial repression
  associated with an undervalued currency,
    38
  easing of, 32, 35, 37–38
  effects of, 36
financial risks, 2–3, 120
financial sector
  accumulation of risks, 59
  misallocation of resources, 120
  reform of, 104–116
fintech firms, 110, 111
firms
  achieving favorable policy treatment, 77
  under central SASAC control multiple
    subsidiaries, 86–87
  with different types of ownership, 43
  disparities within groups of, 48–63
  heterogeneity in performance of, 48
  receiving direct subsidies from the state,
    52
fiscal policy, weak in Japan in the 1990s, 119
fiscal resources, needed by the government,
  127
fixed asset investment, 16*n*, 20*n*, 120*n*
foreign exchange, 36, 37
foreign high-technology companies, state-
  financed acquisition of, 128
Foreign Investment Risk Review
  Modernization Act, in the US, 7–8
foreign ownership, in the financial sector, 96
frontier, per capita development relative to, 4
full convergence approach, predicting
  China's growth, 26
funding, taking the form of equity rather
  than debt, 93
future productivity growth, assessing, 44

GDP
  estimated infrastructure investment as a
    share of, 16*n*

growth
  in 2009–16, 13*n*
  compared with services growth
    (1978–2016), 30*f*
  household disposable income as a share of
    (1992–2015), 31*f*
  private consumption as a share of, 28*f*
  services share of, 29*f*
global commodity prices
  China helping moderate, 10
  cyclical recovery in in 2017, 88
  trends in affecting profitability, 66
global economic and trade growth, weak
    recovery of, 13–14
Global Economic Prospects report (World
    Bank), 45, 46
global economic role, of China, 8–10
global exports, China's peaked in 2015, 14
global financial crisis
  China's growth slowdown since, 3
  economic slowdown after, 7–41
  global recovery weak from, 11*t*, 13–14
  pace of economic convergence slowed
    after, 45
  response to by the Hu-Wen leadership, 17
global financial instability, domestic
    economy contributing to a recurrence
    of, 1
global GDP, 8, 8*n*
globalization, 128, 129
global prosperity, 7
global trade
  crossing international borders, 9–10
  expansion of, 14
  recovered very slowly, 13
  slowing of, 3
  weak recovery of, 120
global value chains, 9, 10
goods and services trade, surplus in, 11
governance, of state-owned enterprises, 117
governance indicators, weakness of, 9
governance reforms, 94–95
governance standards, borrowing, 45
government bureaucrats, undermining
    central reform programs, 125
government consumption, strengthened
    since 2010, 29

gross domestic capital formation, 29*n*
gross fixed capital formation, 20*n*
group chairs, influence on internal capital
    allocation, 76
group companies, 78, 137
growth
  difficulty of rebalancing the sources of, 21
  experiences of more than 100 countries,
    25
  factors affecting, 11*t*
  forecasts, studies offering, 44
  global, 8
  potential, approaches to analyzing, 43–46
  rebalancing the sources of, 22
  slowing
    causes of, 10–11
    contributors to, 4
    exacerbating current economic chal-
      lenges, 122
    in the face of rapidly expanding
      credit, 17
  in the two-decade period 2013–33, 9*n*
Guangzhou-Wuhan line, high-speed pas-
    senger rail, 16
"Guiding Opinion on Deepening the
    Reform of State-owned Enterprises," 87
Guodian Group Corporation, 86*n*

healthcare, government relieving state enter-
    prises of, 72
high-income countries, services share of
    household consumption expenditures,
    32
high-speed passenger rail, as an infrastructure
    investment, 15, 16
historical cost, as the easiest form of valua-
    tion, 137
hospital costs, reimbursement for, 34
households
  carrying out most primary production,
    50*n*
  income
    from businesses, 31*n*
    devoted to consumption gradually
      rising, 35
    growing without direct government
      transfers, 22

as a share of GDP (1992–2015), 31*f*
saving
    data on, 33*n*
    increase in, 13
    more, 35
    rate of, 32, 35
    as a share of after-tax household
        income, 33, 33*f*
    as a share of disposable income, 33*f*
services share of consumption, 32*n*
shifting toward services, 32
housing
    investment, 11*t*
    as largest share of real estate investment,
        15
President Hu Jintao, 17, 57
human capital, 24, 44

IMF. *See* International Monetary Fund
    (IMF)
implicit subsidies, 139*n*, 142
imports, shock of any drop in, 9
import substitution initiative, 17
income levels, rising as critical, 127
income perspective, supporting rebalancing,
    30
indigenous innovation initiative, 17, 18
Industrial and Commercial Bank (ICBC),
    126
industrial firms
    interest payments as a share of pretax
        profits (2006–16), 62*f*
    leverage ratio by ownership (1998–2016),
        61*f*
    share of pretax, preinterest earnings
        absorbed by interest payments, 61
industrial policies, favoring state over private
    and foreign firms, 41
industry, growth of lagging the growth of
    services, 30
industry and construction sector, return on
    assets (2003–16), 55*f*
information transmission, share of private
    investment, 40*f*
infrastructure and housing investment, 11*t*
infrastructure investment
    financial payoff from, 15

official data on, 16*n*
in projects, 79
initial public offerings, 111
interest coverage ratio, inverse of, 61
interest payments, 50, 62*f*
interest rates, 65, 127, 128
international convergence, in Asia, 46–48
International Monetary Fund (IMF)
    China's growth, forecasting, 3
    state-owned land, study of, 136
    zombie firms, study of, 114
    zombie industrial firms, estimates of, 113
inventory, valuation of, 137
investment
    in the electric power industry, 77
    excessive reliance on, 9
    infrastructure goal of, 16
    in infrastructure projects, 79
    placing more in state-owned enterprises, 4
    private relative to state, 120
    rebalancing sources of China's growth
        away from, 10
    in services, by state firms versus private
        firms, 100–101
    share of decreasing, 29
    of state-owned enterprises, 108*f*
    in thermal power generation, 77*n*
    transformation of, 2

Japan
    comparing China to, 119
    convergence toward US per capita income,
        46, 47, 47*f*, 120
    growth rates of, 27
    power of the bureaucracy, 125
    slowdown induced by policy, 119
    zombie firms in, 113*n*
JD.com, 91
Jiang Zemin, 91
job creation, in the service sector, 37

Korea, growth of, 26, 27, 48

labor
    dispersion in returns to, 50*n*
    reallocating to reduce dispersion, 48
labor compensation

data on losses, 53

data on private firms, 53*n*

price indices overstating growth of services, 30*n*

national champions, competing with multinationals, 122

national economic census, 58, 59

National Housing Reform Plan, 71

national income, 28

National Integrated Circuit Investment Fund, 2

negative working capital, defined, 106

net assets (depreciated assets), 90*n*

net exports, falling steadily, 29

network effects, of high-speed rail, 15

net worth, defined, 59

nonbank financial institutions, 106, 125

noncorporatized state-owned industrial enterprises, 86

nonfinancial corporate credit, 60*f*

nonfinancial corporations, credit to, 59

nonfinancial enterprises

flow of loans to by ownership, 105*f*

subsidies to listed, 139

nongovernmental classification, including more than private firms, 121*n*

nonperforming loans

criteria for classifying, 116

reported levels of as understated, 95, 116

universe of, 94*n*

nonstate firms, returns of, 58

nonstate service enterprises, returns of, 59*n*

nontariff barriers, elimination of prior to WTO entry, 83

obstacles to sustained China growth, 9

OECD countries, zombie firms in, 113*n*

OECD Services Trade Restrictiveness Index, 101

oil and natural gas, income from the extraction of, 101

one-child policy in 1980, reinforced the decline of fertility, 23

opening up policy, of the Zhu Rongji era, 17

operating profits, of heavily indebted firms, 125

optimism, reasons for, 127–29

Organization Department of the Chinese Communist Party, appointing top management of SASAC companies, 97

overdue bank loans, classifying as "special mention," 116

"overdue but not impaired" loans, 96, 116

ownership types, returns to capital across, 49

passenger traffic, on the dedicated high-speed rail network, 15

payables, defined, 106

payroll taxes, supporting pension payments, 72

pension fund balance, 73*n*

pension pools, 72, 72*n*, 73

pension schemes, 33–34

pension system, 73

People's Bank of China (central bank)

abolished provincial-level branches, 126

bonds sold into the domestic money market, 36–37

eliminated the cap on bank deposit rates, 36

encouraging more swaps, 93–94

guidelines

on microfinance companies, 106

on the swap program, 94

no longer buying up foreign exchange, 37

purchases of foreign exchange, 12

required reserve ratio for banks, 36, 37

research on the government balance sheet, 134

reserve ratio for small and medium depository institutions, 36*n*

per capita development, relative to the frontier, 4

per capita economic development, low level of in 1978, 27

per capita GDP, compared with the United States, 120

per capita income, measures of, 27, 41

performance gap, between private and state firms, 50

performing loans, 94*n*

PetroChina, 87*n*

planned economy approach of the 1950s, emphasis on scale, 77

political economy constraints, to adopting a more far-reaching reform program, 6
political instability, potential, 9
political interference, reducing in the management of enterprises, 99
pooling, extended to nonstate firms, 73
positive working capital, defined, 108
potential growth, defined, 2n
prices, determining, 1
primary sector, described, 50n
private construction companies, returns of, 79n
private consumption, 28–29, 28f
private consumption expenditure, 22, 29
private firms
  balance sheets improving, 63
  contribution to GDP, 2
  corporate loans flowing to, 105
  decline in share of investment, 106
  efficiency of, 43
  eroding the confidence of, 20–21
  facing few entry restrictions in manufacturing, 75
  gaining access to the domestic equity market, 111
  generating high returns, 120
  growth of investment by, 21
  having positive working capital, 108
  internet and high-tech companies proportion of, 109
  lending to decline in recent years, 109
  leverage ratio, 61f
  making indirect loans to state companies, 108
  offsetting declining access to loans, 106
  performance of, 109n
  reducing barriers to entry, 5, 99
  return on assets, 56n
  revenue per unit of assets, 57
  seizure by the state, 20
  small, financing, 64–65
  versus state-owned enterprises, 49–63
  taking over underperforming state assets, 5
  typically having no retirees, 71
private hotels and restaurants, earnings ten times higher than state counterparts, 74
private industrial firms

average leverage ratio of, 61
  interest payments as a share of pretax profits, 62f
  investing retained earnings and borrowing funds, 62
  return on assets controlled by, 79
private investment
  concentrated in manufacturing, 20
  crowding out of, 111
  deceleration relative to state investment, 19, 19f
  decline in the share of, 41
  rapid rise from 2006 to 2011, 19
  share in modern business services (2012–16), 40f
  slowed in 2012 through 2016, 20
  from 2006–16, 19f
private listed firms, capital allocation by, 76
private property rights, 41, 111, 120
private service sector firms, 39, 58
private steel firms
  adjusted to changing market conditions, 69, 70
  divergence in performance from state firms, 68–69
  investment by, 69n
  return on assets, 69f
  superior performance of, 70
production function approach, estimating future expansion, 43–44
production perspective, on rebalancing, 28, 29
productivity, 12, 46, 49, 76
product mix
  of state and private firms, 64, 66
  of state-owned enterprises, 66–70
product tax, replaced with a value-added tax (VAT), 39
profitable state-owned enterprises, 52, 52n
profit-oriented private firms, investment undertaken by, 2
profits, 108f, 141
promotions
  for group chairs, 76
  for local officials, 115, 125
property rights, 21, 41, 111, 120

public economy, consolidating and developing, 18
public institutions, managed as enterprises, 133*n*
public ownership, 18, 91
public services, 74, 94–95
purchasing power parity, 41*n*

quality of labor, improvements in, 24

real bank deposit rates, 35, 36, 36*n*
real estate and infrastructure investment, 15, 16
real wages, 24
rebalancing process
    from the demand side, 32–38
    from the supply side, 38–41
rebalancing progress, factors explaining, 31–41
rebalancing strategy, 28–31
receivables, defined, 106
reform. *See also* economic reform
    of the financial sector, 104–116
    gradualist approach, current, 127
    not necessitating job elimination in state-owned enterprises, 123
    pace of, 11*t*
registered private firms, 56*n*, 58
regression analysis, of data for countries with super rapid growth, 26
regression to the mean, about cross-national growth rates, 25
renminbi. *See also* currency
    appreciation of, 3, 38–39
    undervaluation of, 13, 17
    value against other currencies, 12
replacement cost, estimating, 137
resource allocation, role of the state in, 2, 16, 41
resource use, 10, 49
restrictions on entry, allowing inefficient state services, 75
restrictive licensing, in the service sector, 100
retirees, 71, 73
retirement
    burden on state-owned enterprises, 72

pattern like a wealthy European welfare state, 25
    raising the age of, 24, 25
return on assets
    of all state enterprises, 54*n*
    calculated as pretax profits divided by assets, 54*n*
    calculation of average, 56
    data on, overstating the efficiency of investment, 15
    data to calculate as readily available, 51*b*
    decline in for state-owned enterprises, 51*b*
    defined, 54
    judging economic performance, 51*b*
    measuring the efficiency of firms, 43, 54–55
    of private service sector firms, 58–59, 58*t*
    as profits plus interest expenses divided by assets, 54*n*
    of state and private industrial enterprises, 57*f*
    of state-owned enterprises by sector, 55*f*
revenue per unit, of assets, 51*b*, 57
revenues, of state-owned enterprises, 55*n*
reversion to the mean, 11*t*, 25–27
rural cooperative medical insurance scheme, 33, 34
rural pension scheme, 33, 34
rural-urban migration, easing restrictions on, 23

SASAC. *See* State-Owned Assets Supervision and Administration Commission of the State Council (SASAC)
saving-investment imbalance, 3, 13
scientific research and technical services, 40*f*
secondary sector, covering industrial and construction firms, 50*n*
second-tier banks, capture by local officials, 96
sectoral composition, changing, 11*t*
sectors, of the economy, 50*n*
Security Law (1995), 104
service sector
    displacing industry as the major source of growth, 20
    effect of eliminating the estimated gap, 80

enterprises, return on assets of central (2005–17), 89*t*

financial performance of state firms administered by, 88–90, 89*t*

firms

increase in the assets and indebtedness of, 90

investment by, 90*n*

global role of, 122

merger program reduced competition, 97

mergers of firms within individual industries, 87

mergers orchestrated by (2015–17), 88*t*

mixed ownership in group companies, 97*n*

responsible for dividing firms into categories, 95

as "the world's largest and most powerful holding company," 87

state-owned banks

largest having no "overdue but not impaired" loans, 116

loans almost exclusively to state firms, 104

loans to money-losing state-owned enterprises, 126

recapitalization of, 104

shrinking role of the largest banks, 104*n*

state-owned Chinese thermal power generators, 76–77

state-owned construction companies, 122

state-owned enterprises

access to bank loans, 41

assets, 135

average return on, 58–59

created by investment controlled by, 79

raising average returns on, 3

raising the return on, 99

rapid expansion in, 79

avoiding layoffs, 71

balance sheets deteriorating, 63

bank credit, claiming large share of, 27

bank lending flowing to, 113

borrowed funds paying interest on previous loans, 62

capital, lower cost of, 64, 121

capital-intensive industries

concentration in more, 121

no longer dominating, 70

central SASAC universe, reduced in, 87–88

classified as commercial under SASAC, 95

Communist Party, serving the interest of, 122

consolidating and strengthening a group of central, 18

corporatized, share of, 82–83

credit

misallocation to, 22

new flowing to, 121

delayed payments to foreign firms, 108*n*

dragging growth down, 4

economic growth

emphasized as a major source of, 18

as an increasing drag on, 50

education and healthcare burdens to local governments, 72

efficiency, declining, 43

efficiency and constraints of, 5

employment

downsizing of, 123

having excess, 71

very different from 20 years earlier, 124

with excess capacity receiving subsidies, 140

exit or privatization of the worst performing, 83

expanded claim on financial resources, 114

expanding claim on bank loans and funding, 108

financial losses, rise in the size of, 51

financial performance, deteriorating, 16

financial support for running schools, 72

financing from banks and capital markets, 120–21

funds flowing to prop up ailing, 100

governance of, improving, 117

heavy industry, less dominant than frequently assumed, 68

housing

relieved of investing in, 72

selling off to employees, 71

income absorbed by interest payments, 61–62, 62f

interest rate advantage relative to private firms, 65

international commodity prices, exposed to fluctuations in, 64

less creditworthy after the global financial crisis, 62

less efficient than private firms, 43

leverage increased in real estate and construction, 63

leverage ratio (1998–2016), 61f

leverage twice that of private companies among service sector firms, 63

liabilities of heavily indebted, reducing, 125

limited liability companies included, 53n

losses, 50, 52t, 56

loss-making, 50–52, 53, 54, 55, 121

lower returns of, 64

mergers among the largest, 86

negative working capital, 108

nonfinancial corporates, increase in the debt in, 59

percent

of all investment in services in 2015, 75

corporatized, 82

losing money in 2016, 55

performance

deteriorating, 41, 50

explaining weaker, 63–78

weakening, 57, 120

private firms

buying up distressed, 92–93

compared to, 49–63

product mix effects on underperformance, 66–70

profitability, deteriorating, 120

profit maximizing behavior, insufficient on the part of the senior management, 75

profits and investment of (2011 and 2015), 108f

programs failing to improve performance of, 96–97

reform

current efforts underperforming, 5

dimensions of the current approach, 81

obstacles to, 122–27

by Premier Zhu Rongji, 71

response to, 123

restructuring, uncertainty associated with, 35n

retained earnings, using, 62

return on assets, 52n

adjusted for subsidies, 141

in industry and services, 41

by sector, 55f

revenue per unit of assets, 57

secondary offerings, dominating, 111

services, providing, 64

shocks, more vulnerable to, 63

social burdens, effects on, 70–74

strategy to reform, failing, 81–97

subset of firms losing large amounts of money, 51–52

subsidies

to large numbers of money-losing, 128

of larger, 142

overstating the financial performance of, 55

to, 142

traditional, converting to limited liability or joint stock companies, 81

underperforming

propping up, 2

in services, 64, 74–75

upstream oil and gas, dominating, 88–89

zombies, highest proportion of, 113

state-owned groups, allocation of capital, 76

state-owned industrial enterprises

average leverage ratio of, 61

broadly defined, 56n

corporatization, 84t–85t

corporatization, time series data for, 82

data, on the number of, 82–83

decline in the number of noncorporatized, 86

interest payments as a share of pretax profits, 62f

leverage ratio of, 112f

likely to be unprofitable, 54
losses of above-scale, 54
losses of below-scale, 54
negative working capital, having, 106
overstating the performance of, 57n
return on assets of, 56, 57, 57f, 83
time series data for the corporatization of, 84t–85t
state-owned land, value of, 78, 136
state-owned machinery, in other countries, 135
state-owned nonfinancial assets, 78, 134
state-owned nonfinancial enterprises
assets of, 136t
average annual real growth of assets of, 78
dividing into two categories, 94
more efficient use of assets in recommended, 136
quantity of assets of, 78
state-owned residential housing, stock of, 71
state-owned service sector firms, in SASAC, 90
state-owned steel enterprises
decline in the share of output of by 2016, 70
investment by, 69n
losses of, 69
relative performance declined, 68
return on assets, 69f
state-owned upstream oil and gas firms, 89n
state ownership, associated with lower returns to capital, 49
state sector
leading role of, 18
Xi preferring "to build a bigger and more powerful," 19
steel, measuring true annual domestic consumption of, 69n
steel industry, 68, 69f. See also state-owned steel enterprises
stock exchanges, companies listed on the Shanghai or Shenzhen, 97
stock market, domestic, 8
strategic objectives, of the Chinese Communist Party, 122
subsidies
to almost half of all state enterprises, 117

to firms responsive to state policy priorities, 53n
implicit, 139n, 142
provided to the pension system, 73
receiving with excess capacity, 140
treating as a revenue, 74
substandard loans, 94n
subway systems, globally making losses, 74
"super rapid" economic growth, countries experiencing episodes of, 26
supply side approach, production function approach as, 44
supply side factors, driving the rebalancing process, 38–41
surplus labor in agriculture, absorption of, 23

Taiwan
converging to about half the per capita GDP level of the United States, 46, 47f
growth in terms of per capita GDP, 48
growth rates of, 27
period of super rapid growth, 26
Taobao e-commerce platform, Alibaba's, 110
tariffs, reduction in prior to WTO entry, 83
tax reforms, reducing discrimination against the tertiary sector, 38
technological frontier, measuring, 44
technology firms, 109
Temasek financial holding company, in Singapore, 87
Tencent private internet company, 91, 109n, 110
term contracts, of workers in state firms, 124
tertiary sector, 38, 50n
thermal electric power generation industry, 76
13th Five-Year Plan (2016–20), detailed objectives for six industry subsectors, 18
top line income, business tax levied on, 39
top ten export market, 9
total factor productivity
decline in, 10, 11, 14
defined, 15
estimating, 51b
future growth of, 44
growth when exports are weak or falling, 14

Premier Zhu Rongji
downsizing and restructuring of state companies starting in 1997–98, 16
market-oriented reforms of, 17
on the power of provincial governors and mayors to command local bank presidents, 126
reform of state firms undertaken by, 82
reforms reduced the burden on state enterprises to maintain employment, 73–74
used debt-to-equity swaps as part of the state enterprise restructuring program, 93

zombie firms
among subsidiaries of SASAC, 90
avoiding, 77–78
capitalization of interest on previous loans, 121
continuing to get bank support locally, 96
definitions for, 113–14
forcing into bankruptcy, 5, 100
IMF study understating, 114
local officials insuring the survival of, 78
not eligible for swaps, 94
not unique to China, 113n
operating indefinitely, 117

Other Publications from the
PETERSON INSTITUTE FOR INTERNATIONAL ECONOMICS

POLICY BRIEFS

POLICY ANALYSES IN INTERNATIONAL ECONOMICS SERIES

* = out of print

Economic Sanctions Reconsidered (2 volumes)
Economic Sanctions Reconsidered: Supplemental Case Histories*   Gary Clyde Hufbauer,
Jeffrey J. Schott, and Kimberly Ann Elliott
1985, 2d ed. Dec. 1990   ISBN cloth 0-88132-115-X/
paper 0-88132-105-2
Economic Sanctions Reconsidered: History
and Current Policy*   Gary Clyde Hufbauer,
Jeffrey J. Schott, and Kimberly Ann Elliott
December 1990   ISBN cloth 0-88132-140-0
ISBN paper 0-88132-136-2
Pacific Basin Developing Countries: Prospects
for the Future*   Marcus Noland
January 1991   ISBN cloth 0-88132-141-9
ISBN paper 0-88132-081-1
Currency Convertibility in Eastern Europe
John Williamson, ed.
October 1991   ISBN 0-88132-128-1
Foreign Direct Investment in the United States,
2d ed.*   Edward M. Graham and Paul R. Krugman
January 1991   ISBN 0-88132-139-7
International Adjustment and Financing: The
Lessons of 1985–1991*   C. Fred Bergsten, ed.
January 1992   ISBN 0-88132-112-5
North American Free Trade: Issues and Recommendations*   Gary Clyde Hufbauer and Jeffrey J.
Schott
April 1992   ISBN 0-88132-120-6
Narrowing the U.S. Current Account Deficit*
Alan J. Lenz
June 1992   ISBN 0-88132-103-6
The Economics of Global Warming
William R. Cline
June 1992   ISBN 0-88132-132-X
US Taxation of International Income: Blueprint
for Reform*   Gary Clyde Hufbauer,
assisted by Joanna M. van Rooij
October 1992   ISBN 0-88132-134-6
Who's Bashing Whom? Trade Conflict in High-
Technology Industries   Laura D'Andrea Tyson
November 1992 ISBN 0-88132-106-0
Korea in the World Economy*   Il SaKong
January 1993   ISBN 0-88132-183-4
Pacific Dynamism and the International Economic System*   C. Fred Bergsten and
Marcus Noland, eds.
May 1993   ISBN 0-88132-196-6
Economic Consequences of Soviet Disintegration*   John Williamson, ed.
May 1993   ISBN 0-88132-190-7
Reconcilable Differences? United States-Japan
Economic Conflict*   C. Fred Bergsten and
Marcus Noland
June 1993   ISBN 0-88132-129-X
Does Foreign Exchange Intervention Work?
Kathryn M. Dominguez and Jeffrey A. Frankel
September 1993   ISBN 0-88132-104-4
Sizing Up U.S. Export Disincentives*
J. David Richardson
September 1993   ISBN 0-88132-107-9
NAFTA: An Assessment*   Gary Clyde Hufbauer
and Jeffrey J. Schott, *rev. ed.*
October 1993   ISBN 0-88132-199-0

Adjusting to Volatile Energy Prices
Philip K. Verleger, Jr.
November 1993   ISBN 0-88132-069-2
The Political Economy of Policy Reform
John Williamson, ed.
January 1994   ISBN 0-88132-195-8
Measuring the Costs of Protection in the United
States   Gary Clyde Hufbauer and
Kimberly Ann Elliott
January 1994   ISBN 0-88132-108-7
The Dynamics of Korean Economic Development   Cho Soon
March 1994   ISBN 0-88132-162-1
Reviving the European Union*
C. Randall Henning, Eduard Hochreiter, and Gary
Clyde Hufbauer, eds.
April 1994   ISBN 0-88132-208-3
China in the World Economy   Nicholas R. Lardy
April 1994   ISBN 0-88132-200-8
Greening the GATT: Trade, Environment,
and the Future   Daniel C. Esty
July 1994   ISBN 0-88132-205-9
Western Hemisphere Economic Integration*
Gary Clyde Hufbauer and Jeffrey J. Schott
July 1994   ISBN 0-88132-159-1
Currencies and Politics in the United States,
Germany, and Japan   C. Randall Henning
September 1994   ISBN 0-88132-127-3
Estimating Equilibrium Exchange Rates
John Williamson, ed.
September 1994   ISBN 0-88132-076-5
Managing the World Economy: Fifty Years
after Bretton Woods   Peter B. Kenen, ed.
September 1994   ISBN 0-88132-212-1
Trade Liberalization and International
Institutions*   Jeffrey J. Schott
September 1994   ISBN 978-0-88132-3
Reciprocity and Retaliation in U.S. Trade Policy*
Thomas O. Bayard and Kimberly Ann Elliott
September 1994   ISBN 0-88132-084-6
The Uruguay Round: An Assessment*
Jeffrey J. Schott, assisted by Johanna Buurman
November 1994   ISBN 0-88132-206-7
Measuring the Costs of Protection in Japan*
Yoko Sazanami, Shujiro Urata, and Hiroki Kawai
January 1995   ISBN 0-88132-211-3
Foreign Direct Investment in the United States,
3d ed.   Edward M. Graham and Paul R. Krugman
January 1995   ISBN 0-88132-204-0
The Political Economy of Korea-United States
Cooperation* C. Fred Bergsten and Il SaKong, eds.
February 1995   ISBN 0-88132-213-X
International Debt Reexamined* William R. Cline
February 1995   ISBN 0-88132-083-8
American Trade Politics, 3d ed.*   I. M. Destler
April 1995   ISBN 0-88132-215-6
Managing Official Export Credits: The Quest for
a Global Regime*   John E. Ray
July 1995   ISBN 0-88132-207-5
Asia Pacific Fusion: Japan's Role in APEC
Yoichi Funabashi
October 1995   ISBN 0-88132-224-5
Korea-United States Cooperation in the New
World Order* C. Fred Bergsten and Il SaKong, eds.
February 1996   ISBN 0-88132-226-1

Who Needs to Open the Capital Account?
Olivier Jeanne, Arvind Subramanian, and John Williamson
April 2012   ISBN 978-0-88132-511-9
Devaluing to Prosperity: Misaligned Currencies and Their Growth Consequences   Surjit S. Bhalla
August 2012   ISBN 978-0-88132-623-9
Private Rights and Public Problems: The Global Economics of Intellectual Property in the 21st Century   Keith E. Maskus
September 2012   ISBN 978-0-88132-507-2
Global Economics in Extraordinary Times: Essays in Honor of John Williamson
C. Fred Bergsten and C. Randall Henning, eds.
November 2012   ISBN 978-0-88132-662-8
Rising Tide: Is Growth in Emerging Economies Good for the United States?   Lawrence Edwards and Robert Z. Lawrence
February 2013   ISBN 978-0-88132-500-3
Responding to Financial Crisis: Lessons from Asia Then, the United States and Europe Now
Changyong Rhee and Adam S. Posen, eds.
October 2013   ISBN 978-0-88132-674-1
Fueling Up: The Economic Implications of America's Oil and Gas Boom   Trevor Houser and Shashank Mohan
January 2014   ISBN 978-0-88132-656-7
How Latin America Weathered the Global Financial Crisis   José De Gregorio
January 2014   ISBN 978-0-88132-678-9
Confronting the Curse: The Economics and Geopolitics of Natural Resource Governance
Cullen S. Hendrix and Marcus Noland
May 2014   ISBN 978-0-88132-676-5
Inside the Euro Crisis: An Eyewitness Account
Simeon Djankov
June 2014   ISBN 978-0-88132-685-7
Managing the Euro Area Debt Crisis
William R. Cline
June 2014   ISBN 978-0-88132-687-1
Markets over Mao: The Rise of Private Business in China   Nicholas R. Lardy
September 2014   ISBN 978-0-88132-693-2
Bridging the Pacific: Toward Free Trade and Investment between China and the United States
C. Fred Bergsten, Gary Clyde Hufbauer, and Sean Miner. Assisted by Tyler Moran
October 2014   ISBN 978-0-88132-691-8
The Great Rebirth: Lessons from the Victory of Capitalism over Communism
Anders Åslund and Simeon Djankov, eds.
November 2014   ISBN 978-0-88132-697-0
Ukraine: What Went Wrong and How to Fix It
Anders Åslund
April 2015   ISBN 978-0-88132-701-4
From Stress to Growth: Strengthening Asia's Financial Systems in a Post-Crisis World
Marcus Noland and Donghyun Park, eds.
October 2015   ISBN 978-0-88132-699-4
The Great Tradeoff: Confronting Moral Conflicts in the Era of Globalization
Steven R. Weisman
January 2016   ISBN 978-0-88132-695-6

Rich People, Poor Countries: The Rise of Emerging-Market Tycoons and their Mega Firms   Caroline Freund, assisted by Sarah Oliver
January 2016   ISBN 978-0-88132-703-8
International Monetary Cooperation: Lessons from the Plaza Accord After Thirty Years
C. Fred Bergsten and Russell A. Green, eds.
April 2016   ISBN 978-0-88132-711-3
Currency Conflict and Trade Policy: A New Strategy for the United States   C. Fred Bergsten and Joseph E. Gagnon
June 2017   ISBN 978-0-88132-711-3
Sustaining Economic Growth in Asia
Jérémie Cohen-Setton, Thomas Helbling, Adam S. Posen, and Changyong Rhee, eds.
December 2018   ISBN 978-0-88132-733-5
The State Strikes Back: The End of Economic Reform in China?   Nicholas R. Lardy
January 2019   ISBN 978-0-88132-737-3

SPECIAL REPORTS

1   Promoting World Recovery: A Statement on Global Economic Strategy*   by Twenty-six Economists from Fourteen Countries
December 1982   ISBN 0-88132-013-7
2   Prospects for Adjustment in Argentina, Brazil, and Mexico: Responding to the Debt Crisis*   John Williamson, ed.
June 1983   ISBN 0-88132-016-1
3   Inflation and Indexation: Argentina, Brazil, and Israel*   John Williamson, ed.
March 1985   ISBN 0-88132-037-4
4   Global Economic Imbalances*
C. Fred Bergsten, ed.
March 1986   ISBN 0-88132-042-0
5   African Debt and Financing*   Carol Lancaster and John Williamson, eds.
May 1986   ISBN 0-88132-044-7
6   Resolving the Global Economic Crisis: After Wall Street*   by Thirty-three Economists from Thirteen Countries
December 1987   ISBN 0-88132-070-6
7   World Economic Problems*
Kimberly Ann Elliott and John Williamson, eds.
April 1988   ISBN 0-88132-055-2
    Reforming World Agricultural Trade*
by Twenty-nine Professionals from Seventeen Countries
1988   ISBN 0-88132-088-9
8   Economic Relations Between the United States and Korea: Conflict or Cooperation?*
Thomas O. Bayard and Soogil Young, eds.
January 1989   ISBN 0-88132-068-4
9   Whither APEC? The Progress to Date and Agenda for the Future*   C. Fred Bergsten, ed.
October 1997   ISBN 0-88132-248-2
10 Economic Integration of the Korean Peninsula   Marcus Noland, ed.
January 1998   ISBN 0-88132-255-5
11 Restarting Fast Track*   Jeffrey J. Schott, ed.
April 1998   ISBN 0-88132-259-8

CPSIA information can be obtained
at www.ICGtesting.com
Printed in the USA
BVHW061100110319
542317BV00033B/2228/P

9 780881 327373